Energy Balance
through the Tao

Energy Balance through the Tao

Exercises for Cultivating Yin Energy

Mantak Chia

Destiny Books
Rochester, Vermont

Destiny Books
One Park Street
Rochester, Vermont 05767
www.InnerTraditions.com

Destiny Books is a division of Inner Traditions International

Originally published in Thailand in 1999 by Universal Tao Publications under the title *Tao Yin*

Library of Congress Cataloging-in-Publication Data

Chia, Mantak, 1944-
Energy balance through the Tao : exercises for cultivating yin energy / Mantak Chia.
p. cm.
Includes index.
ISBN 978-1-59477-059-3
1. Dao yin. 2. Breathing exercises. 3. Holistic medicine. I. Title.
RA781.85.C45 2005
613.7'148—dc22
2005016050

Printed and bound in the United States

10 9 8 7 6 5 4 3 2

Text design and layout by Jon Desautels and Rachel Goldenberg
This book was typeset in Janson, with Present and Futura used as display typefaces

Contents

Acknowledgments

The Universal Tao staff involved in the preparation and production of *Energy Balance through the Tao* extend our gratitude to the many generations of Taoist masters who have passed on their special lineage, in the form of an oral transmission, over thousands of years. We particularly thank Taoist master I Yun (Yi Eng) for his openness in transmitting the formulas of Taoist inner alchemy.

We offer our eternal gratitude to our parents and teachers for their many gifts to us. Remembering them brings joy and satisfaction to our continued efforts in presenting the Universal Tao system.

We express special thanks to Susan Davidson for editorial expertise in producing this edition of *Energy Balance through the Tao*. We wish to acknowledge Lee Holden for assembling the first-draft version of the manuscript. We express our gratitude to Lee Holden and Cheri Sunshine for their writing contributions; also, thanks to Gordon Faulkner for his contribution to the historical summary. We thank Felix Senn for lending his expertise as a Tao Yin Instructor and fitness professional to the process of transcribing the practice into written form.

We gratefully acknowledge the beautiful illustrations contributed by Lucka Lama. We also thank Udon Jandee for his contributions to the book graphics.

Special thanks to Tao Garden resident Tao Yin instructor Colin Campbell for his cheerful and invaluable contributions in revising the Tao Yin exercise instructions. We are also grateful for his many interpretive descriptions of exercise names. These may help the reader to attune to the spirit of many of the exercises. We also thank resident Tao Yin instructor Walter Kellenberger for his counsel in checking details of the exercises.

Special thanks to Dennis Huntington for his efforts in coordinating and integrating all of the new material into the final manuscript. We also express our appreciation for his comprehensive writing contributions.

Finally, we wish to thank our certified instructors, students, and sponsors throughout the world for their ongoing contributions to the Universal Tao system and for preserving the vitality of the Universal Tao practices.

Putting Tao Yin into Practice

The practices described in this book have been used successfully for thousands of years by Taoists trained by personal instruction. Readers should not undertake these practices without receiving personal instruction from a certified instructor of the Universal Tao, because some of these practices, if done improperly, may cause injury or result in health problems. This book is intended to supplement individual training by a Universal Tao instructor and to serve as a reference guide for Universal Tao practices. Anyone who undertakes these practices on the basis of this book alone does so entirely at his or her own risk. Universal Tao instructors can be located at our websites: www.universal-tao.com or www.taoinstructors.org

The meditations, practices, and techniques described herein are *not* intended to be used as an alternative or substitute for professional medical treatment and care. If a reader is suffering from a mental or emotional disorder, he or she should consult with an appropriate professional health care practitioner or therapist. Such problems should be corrected before one starts training.

This book does not attempt to give any medical diagnosis, treatment, prescription, or remedial recommendation in relation to any human disease, ailment, suffering, or physical condition whatsoever.

Chinese medicine and Chi Kung emphasize balancing and strengthening the body so that it can heal itself. The meditations, internal exercises, and martial arts of the Universal Tao are basic approaches to this end. Follow the instructions for each exercise carefully. Also pay special attention to the warnings and suggestions. People who have high blood pressure, heart disease, or a generally weak condition should proceed cautiously, having received prior consent from a qualified medical practitioner. People with venereal disease should not attempt any practices involving sexual energy until they are free of the condition.

The Universal Tao and its staff and instructors cannot be responsible for the consequences of any practice or misuse of the information in this book. If the reader undertakes any exercise without strictly following the instructions, notes, and warnings, the responsibility must lie solely with the reader.

Foreword
Poetry in Motion

DENNIS HUNTINGTON

As you begin your practice of these Tao Yin exercises, you would be well advised to maintain an attitude of poetic sensitivity when studying the instructions and performing the movements. You will be cultivating gentleness while developing strength. Your spine will become more flexible and your tendons and psoas muscles will be imbued with elasticity. The wisdom of your body will awaken with the healthy effects of activating the subtle chemistry within. You will remove blockages to your innate vitality and rejuvenate your body and energy. Improved patterns of physical alignment and movement will recondition your spine and refresh your body by opening chi flow in the meridians. You will discover and train your "second brain" in your abdomen, and you will be able to connect with the life-giving power of the universe.

The inner smile is the key to relaxation. Relaxation is the key to internal power. By relaxing and smiling to your abdomen you activate the abdominal chi. At the same time, you begin to train your feeling and awareness brain in the abdomen, the tan tien, to coordinate and direct the actions in the body.

For thousands of years Taoists have trained their tan tiens in order to use their tan tiens. However, most Western students of the Tao have only superficially understood the practical significance of this training. Focused training of the tan tien second brain is the cornerstone of all the practices that Master Mantak Chia teaches.

In the process of learning the various Tao Yin exercises taught in this book, you also learn to train and develop your Yi, the mind-eye-heart power.

In the process of conditioning your all-important spine and psoas muscles, you also learn to integrate the subtle power of the breath and mind. Then, as you progress through the exercises, you learn to coordinate the network of round muscles throughout the body. When working in sync with the psoas muscles and spine, the pulsing of these "chi muscles" fills the whole body with chi, energizing the body and releasing pleasant sensations. The physical and energetic foundations of your Yi become quite clear.

Part 1 of this book provides background information helpful to your understanding of Tao Yin. The exercises, in Part 2, are organized in five sets. Each of the exercises has its own value; as well, skills from several exercises may be combined to achieve the full measure of success in the more complex movement sequences. Perform the exercises with full awareness and sensitivity; they are moving meditations. Tremendous benefits will follow. Many of the exercises involve retraining your patterns of movement and structural alignment. This initially requires patience and conscientious attention to details, and it is also pleasant and fun.

It is important to do each exercise accurately and in the spirit described in the instructions. Most of the exercises are straightforward, and the mechanics of the movement are easy to grasp. Use a little imagination. Discover and emulate the spirit suggested by the names taken from animals or phenomena in nature. Sense the exercises as poetry in motion. Connect with all levels of the experience.

In the first set of exercises you breathe consciously, with light, in order to release tensions and toxins and to energize tired or weak areas during rest between exercises. You learn to direct the subtle chi breath throughout the body. Conscious breathing deepens the effectiveness of the exercises. You coordinate calm, steady abdominal breathing with movement as you condition and retrain your spine and psoas muscles. You will also learn exercises, breath, and meditation practices for balancing and harmonizing hot and cold energy in the body.

By the time you get to the Cobra's Ritual of Love exercise sequence in chapter 9, you will be combining your skills to achieve a more profound internal, energetic experience. You will have begun to acquire the fundamentals of conditioning and inner sensing. When you integrate the mechanics of the Love Cobra with internal dynamics and awareness, you will enjoy a sweet reward for your efforts. This will enable you to combine correct body movement, internal forces, breath, chi, and Yi for a pleasant and full-body flowering of your energy.

The heightened awareness experienced in the Love Cobra will also serve you in your approach to other exercises, helping you to achieve their benefits more fully. Discover and sense the spirit. Experience the poetry of each exercise.

The Empty Force Breath practice is introduced after you have had time to gain a sense of ease and familiarity with many of the exercises. The Empty Force Breath exercises remove stagnant abdominal chi and greatly increase body oxygen. The Empty Force Breath techniques can be combined with other Tao Yin exercises to increase their benefits.

The last set of exercises begins with the dynamic principle of finding the straight vector in the curve. Exercises such as the Dragon Stretches Tail series use this principle to grow and strengthen tendons and to cultivate their elasticity. These sitting exercises are integrated with spinal and psoas movements. Then tendons in the fingertips, arms, neck, and scapulae through the length of the spine and in the lower back to the legs are stretched. They become unified as one seamless tendon, releasing tensions and blockages; this is followed by a soothing, calm, energizing efflorescence of chi. The practice section concludes with a delightful variety of light exercises for the spine, shoulders, and back.

The Tao Yin exercises included in this book are all performed in either lying or sitting positions. As such, they provide unique benefits that cannot be so readily achieved in standing or moving practices. The conditioning and health benefits engendered in Tao Yin stand on their own merits. Any person from any background or belief system can receive the benefits of the practice. Tao Yin is also an excellent preparation for any other activity one may pursue—whether it be sports, martial arts, music, meditation, work, or just plain living.

Tao Yin translates as "energy directing," but this does not refer to directing energy in the meridians during the active phases of performing the exercises. Rather, the chi flow is opened in the meridians during the passive, resting phase as a result of performing the exercises correctly. One does not need prior knowledge of chi meridians in order to enjoy the benefits of this practice; however, meridian information is provided for reference at many of the exercises. An appendix provides further information on the meridians.

With the body deeply relaxed, the mind calm, the tan tien full of chi, and chi flowing in the meridians, your finish with the crème de la crème, the Yin Meditation. You set the stage for this deeply satisfying and sometimes profound experience of the life energy by preparing your body with all of the previous Tao Yin exercises. You might experience the fullness of a delightful yang "cell massage," a refreshing emotional cleansing, or the refined yin state of embryonic breathing.

Though Tao Yin stands on its own as an independent form of practice, it is also part of an overall system of practices in the Universal Tao system. Each part of the Universal Tao system is valuable by itself and at the same time benefits and is benefited by other practices. Refer to page 200 for a summary of the Universal Tao system and contact information for practice support.

Dennis Huntington is a resident instructor at the Universal Tao Training Center at Tao Garden Health Resort in Thailand. He began training with Master Mantak Chia in 1986 and became a certified Universal Tao instructor in 1992.

導引
Tao Yin

PART 1
Foundations

Tao, chi, man, nature, and universe. This image depicts the "protective animals" that represent the essence of energy of the vital organs. The eight forces of nature found in the pakua (thunder/lightning, wind, water, fire, heaven, earth, rain/lake, and mountain) are present. The energetic forces of the universe are represented, and in the midst of it all a human is connected to the infinite power of the universe. The three tan tiens—the tan tien of the head, the heart, and the lower abdomen—are activated by the gentle, joyful inner smile. The inner world is connected and at peace with the outer world.

Man, Nature, the Universe, and Tao Yin

Tao Yin is a form of energy-enlivening exercise originating out of Taoism, China's oldest philosophical system. An integral part of the Universal Tao practice, Tao Yin is a series of revitalizing exercises that develop flexibility, strength, resiliency, and suppleness. Through their integrative principles these exercises create harmony within the body, mind, and spirit, leading one to discover balance within nature and a way to move freely within the ebb and flow of life's ceaseless current.

Since prerecorded history, men and women in China have studied the essential harmony between humans and nature. These people call themselves Taoists. Taoists see humans as living organisms within a larger living organism—nature—which itself exists within an even larger living organism: the universe. *Tao* means "the way": the way of humans, the way of nature, the way of the universe, and the way to merge into the essential harmony of all things. Tao is the way to the source of life, the Wu Chi: the formless, undifferentiated energy that permeates all creation. Taoists place their attention on the invisible energetic force that gives all of these organisms life.

The earliest Taoists discovered that there is no separation between the physical, emotional, psychological, and spiritual selves; whatever happens to us on any of these levels affects us on all other levels as well. The body, mind, and spirit are intimately related, as they are all unique aspects of the same source of energy. So if we are emotionally overstressed, for example, that stress will manifest itself in the body as physical symptoms. If we abuse or neglect our physical body, there will be very real effects on us psychologically and emotionally.

3

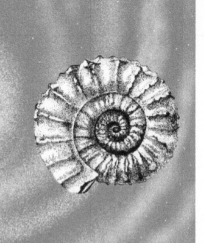

Spiral energy pattern. Energy in nature commonly flows in a spiral pattern. Our Milky Way galaxy and two-thirds of the galaxies in the universe are "spirallic." Hurricanes and tornadoes form a spiral pattern around an axis. Here we see the spiral pattern etched in the formation of a common snail shell.

The Chinese call life-force energy *chi*. Chi circulates through the body in specific pathways, preserving the integrity of the body, mind, and spirit. Chi is the force of vitality at work in the world, in nature, and in the human body. For Taoist doctors, health means more than simply the condition of the different parts of the physical body. Taoists understand sickness as a block in the circulation of chi in the body.

In order to increase the circulation of chi, the early Taoists developed exercises and meditations that reflected the processes they observed in nature. They observed that nature never wastes anything. Everything in nature is always conserved, recycled, and transformed. The exercises and meditations that you will learn in this book allow us to conserve our own vital life force, recycle it through our bodies, and transform any toxic or unbalanced energy into pure and positive energy.

TAO YIN, "ENERGY DIRECTING"

The name of this system of exercises is Tao Yin, 導引; the Chinese name translates as "energy directing." The word *yin* in this name is not the same as the yin that we know of in English as an element of the yin yang symbol 陰 陽. That symbol represents the interaction of the energy of life's complementary polar opposites, such as cold and hot; the Chinese character for *yin*, which means "cold," is a single character. The Yin in Tao Yin is a combination of two Chinese characters. The first character 導 represents the Taoist concept of mind-eye-heart power, Yi (pronounced "ee"). The second character 引 means "directing," and the pronunciation is translated into

English as "in." Hence, the characters for Yi and In combine to become Yin, meaning "mind-eye-heart–power directing." When shown with the character for Tao, the translation is roughly "directing chi using mind-eye-heart power."

The practice of "energy directing" as taught in this book is used to release chronic tension, energy blockages, and toxicity that may have accumulated in your body over many years. *Tao* refers to the fact that physical movements are guided by the strength of the mind and in turn stimulate the internal flow of chi within the body; *Yin* means that chi can reach the bodily extremities with the aid of physical movements. The Tao Yin exercises activate chi flow in the meridians, opening and strengthening them. In this way, the flow of chi from the tan tien (the central chi storage area, located in the lower abdomen) links the yin and yang meridians of the body before returning to its starting point. (The yin meridians are deeper and more internal, whereas the yang meridians are near the outer surfaces of the body and in areas of the extremities.)

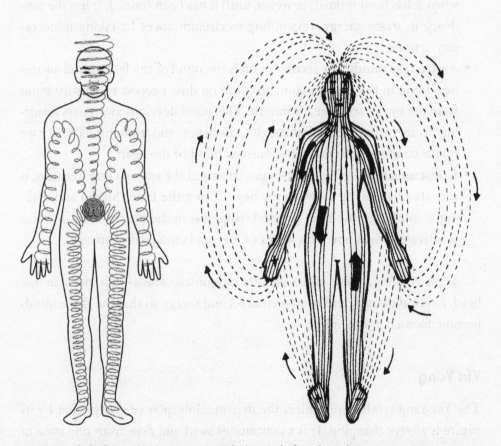

Patterns of chi flow. The figure on the left shows chi flow from the tan tien storage center to the body's extremities. The figure on the right suggests an overall pattern extending out from the extremities and returning back into the body.

Tao Yin, part of Chinese traditional medical literature, is among the practices characterized as "nourishing the vital principle." Doctors in China prescribe certain Tao Yin exercises to heal chronic or acute health problems and to prevent them.

Yi

In this Tao Yin context, "strength of mind" in its fullest sense means Yi, mind-eye-heart power. Yi is the combined force of three minds, or centers of consciousness: the observation mind, the awareness mind, and the conscious mind.

- **Observation mind:** The first mind is the mind of the brain and the inner eye (the third eye). It is capable of accessing a state of higher consciousness and also has access to information received through the eyes, ears, nose, and mouth. This mind may be considered the "observation mind" when it has been trained; however, until it has been trained, it has the tendency to waste energy, responding to circumstances by taking unnecessary actions.
- **Awareness mind:** The second mind is the mind of the feeling and awareness brain in the lower abdomen; it has no direct access to sensory input from the eyes, ears, nose, or mouth. This mind develops awareness resulting from feeling gained through experience and training. These two minds combine with the consciousness mind of the heart.
- **Conscious mind:** The heart-brain, known as the seat of consciousness, is activated by smiling down to the heart (using the Inner Smile) and making it soft by feeling love, joy, and happiness in the heart. Consciousness is activated when one feels waves of love and compassion energy.

With training, these three centers of consciousness—tan tiens in the head, lower abdomen, and heart—connect and merge so that the three minds become focused as one mind.

Yin Yang

The Yin Yang symbol epitomizes the dynamic interplay of energy that by its nature is always changing. It is a continuous swirl and flow from one state of a polar opposite to the other—hot to cold, wet to dry, light to dark, positive to negative, and back again. The same interplay of energies occurs in our own

The yin yang symbol

bodies, including the energy of our emotions—love and hate, happiness and grief, fulfillment and longing.

In addition to the patterns of chi flow within our bodies, there is also external chi that affects our bodies. The Chinese characterized the chi of the heavens as yang: outward flowing, expansive, positively charged; they characterized the earth chi as yin: inward flowing, receptive, negatively charged. Generally speaking, energy flows up the front of the body from the earth, flowing up the inside of the legs and arms toward the heavens. Correspondingly, energy flows down from the heavens, flowing down the back and down the outside of the arms and legs to the earth. Through these polarities man and woman walk erect.

This external pattern of chi flow should not be confused with the body's internal meridian patterns. The body has its own directional map. Yin meridians of the hands flow down the arms. The Stomach meridian on the front of the body flows downward while the Governor meridian flows upward on the back. There are many patterns of chi flow in and around us.

While it is good to have a general awareness of chi flow, one does not need to know the meridians of the body to be a successful practitioner of Tao Yin. "Energy directing" does not mean directing chi in the meridians while doing the postures. Rather, during the active phase of a Tao Yin exercise the student should concentrate on performing the postural movements correctly. The focus should be on applying and directing physical force accurately. Don't think that you are directing chi in the meridians. The chi will be activated and strengthened in the affected meridians as a result of doing the exercise correctly. Chi will flow during the passive phase of rest between exertions.

Why is it beneficial to stretch the body in the manner that we do in Tao Yin exercises? Stretching brings energy from the interior of the body to the

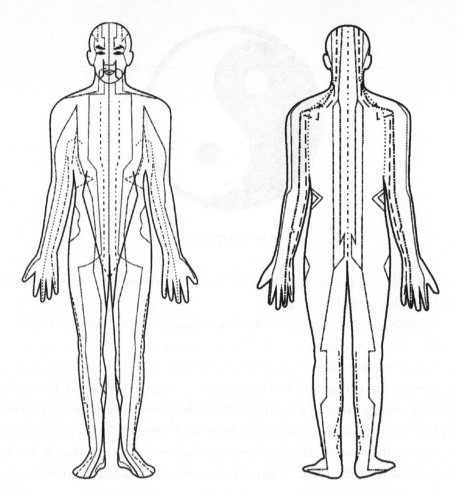

Chi from heaven and earth. Yin earth energy flows up the front of the body from the earth toward the heavens. Yang heavenly chi flows down the back from the heavens to the earth.

exterior, lengthening the meridians and bringing chi to the surface. This allows the energy to flow easily and where it needs to, balancing the chi and restoring health to the organism. By working progressively through the Tao Yin exercises and engaging most of the meridians, the benefits are multiplied throughout the whole body.

Meridians can become blocked by physical, mental, or emotional toxins and tensions. Just like a dam that blocks a river, that blockage stops the flow of life energy and creates stagnation. Above the dam the flow builds up to excess while below the dam the riverbed or channel is nearly empty, with little flow. This imbalance leads to sickness and ill health. By loosening and stretching the meridians, the energy flows freely, allowing healing energy to permeate the whole body.

POSTURES, MOVEMENTS, AND CHI

There are many postures and movements in Tao Yin exercises. The emphasis is always on achieving a state of harmony between body and mind. Tao Yin focuses on growing the tendons, relaxing the psoas muscle and the diaphragm, developing strength and flexibility in the body, releasing toxins through the breath, and training the second brain in the lower tan tien (lower abdomen) to coordinate and direct these processes. The goal of Tao Yin, as with all Chinese internal arts, is to guide and harmonize chi.

Chi is the vital power of the Tao at work in the world: in nature, in society, and in the human body. It is a continuously changing, forever flowing force, an energy that can appear and disappear, can be strong and weak, can be controlled and can also be overwhelming. Chi is what moves on, what transforms qualitatively in the changing rhythm of the seasons; chi shines in rays of the sun. The quality and balance of chi flow is what constitutes health or sickness in the body. Chi affects how we live, move, eat, and sleep.

The goal of all physical practice is to guide and harmonize chi. To guide means to control, to strengthen, to increase or decrease. To harmonize is to free, to open up the energy channels and be in accord with nature. To become aware of this flow of energy throughout the body, to learn to feel it, regulate it, and open the meridian channels to encourage its perfectly smooth flow is another important step in the physical practices of the aspiring Taoist.

The Tao Yin exercises in this book use a specific style of movement to direct energy into the tendons. Certain postures, as well as emotional balancing of the heart and kidneys, will relax the spine and the muscles of the psoas complex, an important pair of muscles that originate on the lower spine, pelvic bones, and hip bones and that connect to the femur bones in the upper legs. Relaxing the psoas muscles allows energy to be directed into the thoracic area and diaphragm. Breathing and intention are also used to release toxins that have accumulated in the body.

The ultimate goal of practicing Tao Yin energy-directing exercises is to become soft, pure, responsive, and full of energy, like a child. Tao Yin can be used for physical, emotional, and spiritual cultivation. Although these exercises are surprisingly simple to perform, they are sophisticated and effective in re-establishing the harmony we have lost between ourselves, nature, and the universe. People from all walks of life use Tao Yin for personal development.

Man, Nature,
the Universe,
and Tao Yin

The History of Tao Yin

Today in China, as in the past, people from various backgrounds gather in the parks at dawn to revitalize their bodies and minds. They also come in hopes of gaining longevity. As darkness disperses with the energizing rays of the rising sun, they perform a variety of exercises that are as rich, diverse, and ancient as Chinese culture itself.

Tao Yin exercises have blossomed out of the traditions of Chinese medicine, martial arts, and the spiritual practices of Taoism and Buddhism. Chi, the bioelectromagnetic life force, is a common thread that connects these various practices. Whether the exercise forms came out of the martial arts tradition, the spiritual path, the military, or medicinal practices, the goal of cultivating, refining, and building chi reserves has remained a constant.

Tao Yin and Chi Kung are the names by which the exercises in this book are most widely known. Spanning a history of over five thousand years, these exercise forms have had many names: Tao Yin, Tao-In, Daoyin, Chi Kung, Qiqong, and Qi Gong are the most common transliterations that a contemporary English reader might have come across. There are many transcribed names, such as Xingqi (Syingchi), Liandan, Xuangong (Syangong), Jinggong, Dinggong, Xinggong (Syingong), Neigong, Xiudao (Syiudao), Zuoshan (Dzwoshan), Neiyang Gong, and Yangsheng Gong, to name a few—the variations determined by the tradition or style of practice the names are associated with. It was not until 1953 when Liu Guizheng (Gweijeng) wrote and published *Practice on Qigong Therapy* that Qigong (Chigong, Chi Kung) became recognized as the formal name for this field of practice. Even the transcribed spelling of Chi Kung varies depending on what tradition or transcription system one is using. (Other spellings include Qiqong and Qi Gong.)

In fact, there are several transcription systems. The Wade-Giles system

The Chinese character for longevity

(W/G) prevailed from 1859–1912 and is still favored by many. The Pinyin system (PY) of transcription for romanizing Chinese-language words and expressions was adopted by the Chinese government as the official standard and has been in use in the People's Republic of China since 1958. These are the two major transcription systems that have provided the English-reading world with recognizable English-looking words to represent Chinese names, words, expressions, and concepts.

There are problems with both systems with regard to matching the sounds of Chinese to the sounds of English, however. Even when transcribing the official Chinese dialect, Mandarin, Wade-Giles and Pinyin transcribe Chinese into English using words that appear to have entirely different meanings. Both systems have provided words that many of us have come to recognize, but neither system consistently uses English phonetic sounds that closely resemble the spoken sounds of Chinese. To be sure, there are many difficulties inherent in the transcription process, because English and Chinese come from very different language systems of speaking and writing.

Nevertheless, the Yale transcription system attempts to bridge the language gap by using standard sounds of English to approximate the spoken sounds of Chinese. For many of the words in this chapter we include the Yale version in parentheses next to the Wade-Giles or Pinyin transcriptions.

Tao Yin is the name that we have elected to use for the system of exercises in this book. The Pinyin version is Daoyin. While the Pinyin system is used in the People's Republic of China, many terms transcribed in the Wade-Giles system are more familiar to the general English-reading public. *Chi Kung* (Wade-Giles) is actually pronounced "chi gung," with the *u* sounded as the *ou* in "you"). *Tao* and *Taoism* are rendered as *Dao* and *Daoism* in Pinyin transcription. The English pronunciation for *ch'i* ("chi") and *ch'i kung* ("chi kung") in Wade-Giles is more straightforward than "qi" or "qigong." People who haven't studied Pinyin are not likely to know that *q* is actually pronounced "ch," as in "church" in the Pinyin system of pronunciation.

In Wade-Giles, the Chinese sound for *t*, as in *Tao*, is the *d* sound; while the word is spelled with a *t*, those in the know say "dao." In order to keep it simple and to remain consistent with conventions used in our existing publications, we chose to stay with *Tao* and *chi* from the Wade-Giles transcription system. On the other hand, we will opt to use words we like that have come into common usage in English, regardless of the system from which any one was derived. In the words of the famous American poet Walt Whitman, "If I contradict myself, then I contradict myself!" Things change—that's the Tao. (Say it with a *d:* "Dao"!)

HEALTH, PREVENTION, AND LONGEVITY

Tao Yin is one of the oldest and most diverse forms of exercise in Chinese history; it holds an important position in the traditional Chinese arts of preserving one's health. The exercises known as Tao Yin are used as preventives against symptoms of old age and sickness; they are also used to cure certain diseases, both chronic and acute. Tao Yin is often classified as either part of traditional medical knowledge or among the various practices of Yangsheng, also known as Zhisheng (Jrsheng). In the second century B.C.E. writings of the *Zhuangzi (Chuangdz)*, the practices of "nourishing the vital principle" were dated to the fourth century B.C.E. The practices amount to a way of life according to psychophysical principles of cultivating energy.

> To pant, to puff, to hail, to sip, to spit out the old breath and draw in the new, practicing bear-hangings and bird-stretchings, longevity his only concern—such is the life favored by the scholar who practices gymnastics, the man who nourishes his body, who hopes to live to be as old as Pengzu, for more than eight hundred years.

From the time of the *Zhuangzi (Chuangdz)* until the present, these physical exercises ("gymnastics," as they are sometimes translated) have played a significant role in Chinese culture and medicine. Early records of these exercises were found in hidden tombs, written on bamboo slips, and carved in stones. Yet the majority of these early exercises have been transmitted in the

Taoist Canon (Daozang) (Daodzang), a compilation of many Taoist practices, exercises, philosophies, and meditations edited in the Ming dynasty (1368–1644). However, before that, on some copperware from the Shang dynasty (1766–1122 B.C.E.) and the Western Zhou (Jou) dynasty (1122–771 B.C.E.), there are pictures that vividly show various postures of ancient people doing Tao Yin exercises. This shows that Chi Kung and Tao Yin came into existence long before the invention of written language.

In the eighth century B.C.E., the Western Zhou (Jou) dynasty went out of existence. The Eastern Zhou (Jou) was divided into two periods, the Spring and Autumn Period (770–476 BC) and the Warring States Period (475–221 BC), during which one hundred schools of thought contended, pushing Chi Kung to a high theoretical level. It was in this latter period that Tao Yin developed into a fairly systematic art for the preservation of health. The scholar Lao Tzu (Lao Dz), to whom the *Tao Te Ching* (Classic of the Way of Power) is ascribed, suggested a method of health preservation by regulating respiration. One book compiled during this period, *Huangdi (Hwangdi) Neijing* (The Yellow Emperor's Classic of Internal Medicine), contains records of Chi Kung, many of which deal with methods of practice, symptoms, effects, and points for attention. In the book a dialogue between Huangdi (Hwangdi) and Qi (Chi) Bo, a renowned doctor, stresses the combination of medical treatment with Tao Yin exercises.

China was unified by the First Emperor, Qin Shi Huangdi (Chin Shr Hwangdi), of the Qin (Chin) dynasty (221–207 B.C.E.). To strengthen his rule, the emperor ordered the burning of books other than those approved by the Qin (Chin) government. Soon after this, even the books kept in the royal palace were destroyed in the war with Liu Bang, founder of the Han dynasty (206 B.C.E.–220 C.E.). Fortunately, some of the classics escaped these disasters and were buried as sacrificial objects in a tomb in Changsha, which was discovered in 1974. These are well preserved in the form of bamboo slips and silk paintings, including forty-four Tao Yin diagrams of *Tao Yin Tu* (Tao Yin Exercises Illustrated). There are also copies of the Tao Te Ching, the I Ching, and some medical books, all of great value for the study of Chi Kung.

Tao Yin developed further during the Han dynasty, when it received widespread recognition. Many texts were written in this period, such as *Zhuangzi (Chuangdz)* (Book of Master Chuang), written around 200 B.C.E., and *Huainanzi (Hwainandz)* (Book of the Hwainan Master), written under the patronage of Liu An, grandson of the first emperor of the Han dynasty. Of special importance to the internal work of Chi Kung is *Cantongqi (Cantongchi)* (The Kinship of the Three), written by Wei Boyang.

This last treatise, concerning Wei Boyang's alchemist's knowledge and personal experience in health preservation, contains a twelve-section Tao Yin Brocade and a Seven Stars standing routine. Hua Tuo (Hwa Two) (141–208 C.E.), staff physician of Cao Cao (Tsao Tsao) (ruler of the kingdom of Wei) and a personage held in high esteem in the Chinese medical world, created Wuqinxi (Wuchinsyi), Five Animal Play, a Tao Yin exercise that imitates the movements of tigers, deer, bears, apes, and birds and that is still popular across China today. A copy of this exercise is contained in *Taishang Laojun (Laojwen) Yangsheng Jue (Jwe)* (Formulas on Nourishing Life of the Highest Venerable Lord).

Xu Xun (Syu Sywen) (239–374 C.E.) was a regular practitioner of Tao Yin exercises. He was called Xu (Syu), the true master, and lived to the age of 136. His art of Tao Yin was later summarized into a most popular book entitled *Ling Jianzi (Jiandz)* (Miraculous Swordsmanship). Ge Hong (281–341), author of *Zhouhou (Jouhou) Beijifang* (Handbook of Prescriptions for Emergencies) and the *Baopuzi (Baopudz)*, said that Chi Kung exercises were meant to "cure diseases beforehand and achieve harmony among all elements."

The greatest innovation in the field of therapeutic Tao Yin occurred in 610 when Chao Yuanfang (550–630), a doctor of the Imperial Medical Academy, published his *Zhubingyuan Houlun (Jubingyuan Houlwen)* (Treatise on the Causes and Symptoms of Diseases) in five volumes. This work contained many quotations from *Yangsheng Fang* (Methods for Nourishing Life), 1,139 medical discussions, and some 213 Tao Yin exercises classified in accordance with the origins and symptoms of given medical conditions.

In 652, during the Tang dynasty, Sun Simiao (Szmiao) (581–682), a renowned physician, compiled the *Qianjin (Chianjin) Yaofang* (Prescriptions of a Thousand Ounces of Gold) in which he introduced a number of therapeutic exercises based on Chi Kung, notably the Liuzijue (Liudzjwe). It was in the Tang dynasty that Tao Yin became an official part of the court medicine and was generally in the hands of the massage specialist.

In the late Qing (Ching) dynasty, Chi Kung began to decline. Some books on Chi Kung were published in the early days of the Republic of China (1911–1949), although, with the exception of Jiang Weiqiao's (Weichiao's) 1914 book, *Yinshizi Jingzuofa (Yinshrdz Jingdzwofa)* (Master Yinshr's Quiet Sitting Methods), most were of little value. As a whole, however, Chi Kung was neglected and on the verge of extinction. Fortunately, it was brought back to life in the early 1950s, when the Chinese government organized comprehensive research into Chi Kung.

ANIMALS AND TAO YIN

Among all the gymnastic exercises that are considered useful in therapy and in the prevention of diseases, the Five Animals Pattern is the most popular. It is generally attributed to Hua Tuo, staff physician of Cao Cao (Tsao Tsao) under the Three Kingdoms. According to his official biography in *Sanguo Zhi (Sangwo Jr)* (Record of the Three Kingdoms), he outlined the concepts underlying their practice to his disciple Wu Pu.

> The body needs a certain amount of movement. This movement serves to properly balance right and left . . . it causes the blood to circulate properly and prevents the origination of diseases.
>
> The human body is like a door hinge that never comes to rest. This is why Taoists practice gymnastics. They imitate the movements of the bear, which hangs itself head-down from a tree; of the owl, which keeps turning its head in different ways. They stretch and bend the waist and move all the joints and muscles of their bodies to evade aging.
>
> I also have developed a series of exercises which I name the Five Animal Pattern. The five animals are the tiger, the deer, the bear, the monkey, and the bird. The practice of the Pattern aids the elimination of diseases and increases the functioning of the lesser members. Whenever a disorder is felt in the body, one of the Animals should be practiced until one perspires freely.

Most of the exercises in this book are part of the Animal Pattern of Tao Yin. For example, there are several different Monkey series of exercises: Plays on Ground (six exercises), Sitting on a Rock Ready to Jump (two exercises), and five other Monkey exercises. Why so many Monkey exercises? It might be because of the infamously ever restless and active "monkey mind." The monkey entertains itself, finding different ways to manipulate its body—the monkey is a very clever creature. It may also be because we are of similar design.

Some other names of exercises reflect other movements in nature. The idea is that by emulating those movements in a natural way in the body, we are harmonizing ourselves with the natural flow of forces within us. Note exercise names such as River Flows into the Valley and Bamboo Swinging in the Wind. By achieving balance and harmony with the natural forces within, we can more easily harmonize with natural forces around us.

Sense the delicacy, control, and balance implied by the exercise name Cricket Rests on Flower. Feel the power and stability of Mountain Rises from Sea. Try the Cobra's Ritual of Love and the Hummingbird exercises.

Sit like a Tiger Resting in Shade. By catching the spirit observed in the natural flow of energy in a movement in nature or in certain animals, we can learn to do the movement correctly ourselves. Taoists respect creatures of the animal kingdom for the strength and elasticity of their bodies and for their vital energy. All of the Tao Yin exercises are designed to open the body and to cultivate an abundance of energy.

By being close observers of nature, Taoists past and present have established a common ground on which the Tao Yin practices can be shared. We can look to nature to get the idea of and some insight into the performance of the exercises. We can look into ourselves with a relaxed, smiling attitude to discover the benefits of doing them correctly.

3

Tao Yin and the Universal Tao System

The Universal Tao is a practical system of self-development, giving students and practitioners inner and outer resources for enhancing their lives. Tao Yin, an integral part of the Universal Tao system, provides fundamental training of the body, mind, and spirit using yogalike postures. In the Universal Tao we practice a combination of lying, sitting, standing, and moving practices that mutually support one another. The resulting synergy creates a strong foundation for mastering the full gamut of the internal arts.

The Tao Yin basic exercises in this book are lying and seated practices that open the body in ways that, for the most part, can only be done on the floor or on a comparable surface. A mat is recommended. In fact, Tao Yin is a form of moving exercise and meditation that is extremely valuable in its own right, but is also designed to enhance the rest of the Universal Tao practices.

TAO YIN: INTEGRAL PART OF THE COMPLETE TAOIST PRACTICE

Tao Yin is an important part of the Taoist system as a whole. It is a form of moving meditation that relaxes the body, opens the meridians, and clears the mind. The ancient Taoists discovered the vital importance of working with all of our internal resources and the importance of being able to tap into that wealth of potential within. Many practitioners of Tai Chi, Chi Kung, and the martial arts use Tao Yin as a way to open the body in order to move with more internal power.

The Taoist system uses a combination of lying, sitting, standing, and moving exercises to create a highly effective practice for cultivating internal energy. While there are wonderful standing and moving sequences of Tao Yin practice, only lying and sitting positions are used in this book of basic Tao Yin exercises. These exercises, beneficial in their own right, are quite effective complements to the standing and moving practices of Chi Kung and Tai Chi. The pictures below show some of the Tao Yin movements taught in this book.

All of the Taoist practices mutually support one another as a way to delve deeper into our inner potentials. For example, Tao Yin is great way to warm up before engaging in any of the Universal Tao meditation techniques. Relaxing the body, opening the meridians, and calming the mind are essential to going into deep meditation. Tao Yin also helps to refine the practice of

Tao Yin floor exercise Peacock Looks at Its Tail: Conditions spine, tendons, and psoas muscle

Tao Yin floor exercise Monkey Prays with Elbows: Balances energy, conditions spine and psoas muscles

Tao Yin sitting posture Pull Bow and Shoot Arrow: Stretches and grows the tendons

Tao Yin develops the structure of the body and so benefits the practice of both Tai Chi and Chi Kung. On the left is a tai chi movement; the movement on the right is called Pulling the Beaks, part of Iron Shirt Chi Kung's Golden Phoenix Washes Its Feathers.

both Tai Chi and Chi Kung by developing the structure of the body, the strength of the tendons, and a deep connection to the center of the body, the tan tien and the second brain. Tao Yin is a foundation practice. Use it as a stepping stone into yourself, discovering unity of movement, alignment of the body, and the flow of powerful energy through the entire being. For more information on specific Universal Tao practices and meditations, contact the Universal Healing Tao Center. See page 201 for contact information.

THE PRINCIPLES OF TAO YIN

These Tao Yin exercises and meditations are performed on the floor rather than standing. Lying and sitting positions bring about unique benefits: the conditioning that can be achieved improves health and structural alignment, strengthening the body for performing movements and postures in standing positions. The principles of movement in Tao Yin practice are essentially the same as in Iron Shirt Chi Kung and Tai Chi, allowing the three forms of exercise to mutually support one another. The basic principles of Tao Yin, Iron Shirt Chi Kung, and Tai Chi are to promote relaxation, energy flow, centering, resiliency, and enjoyment.

Relaxation is the first principle of the internal arts. Without relaxation the body is tight and tense and the mind is scattered and confused. The ancient Taoists discovered that relaxation is a way to develop suppleness and power like that of water. Holding tension in the body drains our energy. Relaxation frees up our energy, bringing us health and vitality.

Energy, or chi, is the root of all the internal arts and Taoist practices. Chi is the animating force of the universe. It is the force that allows the planets, stars, and galaxies to work in perfect harmony. It is the force that creates movement within the body, consciousness in the mind, and unity in the spirit. By working with chi, the Taoists discovered the intimate connection between ourselves, nature, and the entire universe. Tao Yin is one very effective way of cultivating more energy in the body, mind, and spirit.

Moving from the center of the body is a theme common to Tao Yin, Chi Kung, and Tai Chi. Tao Yin releases tension and tightness in order to access the center of the body. It is extremely difficult to move from the center of the body when the lumbar area of the spine is tense, the psoas muscles are contracted, and the energy in the lower tan tien is depleted. Because it releases tightness that prevents us from accessing the center of the body, Tao Yin is a foundational set of exercises for the practices of Tai Chi and Chi Kung.

Finally, Tao Yin develops resiliency—a combination of strength and flexibility within the body. Without flexibility the body becomes tense and rigid and without strength the body has no power or alignment. Tao Yin focuses on balancing and harmonizing strength with flexibility.

Tao Yin also facilitates Tai Chi and Chi Kung by developing the alignment and structure of the body. Many people practice Tai Chi and Chi Kung without using proper body mechanics. Practicing Tao Yin exercises will dramatically improve one's Tai Chi and Chi Kung. This happens as a result of aligning the spine, breathing consciously, and conditioning the psoas muscle, and by concurrently training the second brain in the lower tan tien to coordinate these functions and thereby to direct movement and force from the center of the body.

The most important principle of Tao Yin is enjoyment. These exercises are designed to create more joy in life. While practicing Tao Yin, smile. Smiling creates a sense of freedom and relaxation in the body and mind. Have fun as you create a beautiful and powerful body.

These relatively simple Tao Yin practices have very profound effects.

Foundations

The Microcosmic Orbit with energy points and the tan tien energy center

Tao Yin sitting posture Dragon Stretches Tail, Claws Up: Activates chi to flow from sacrum to crown

TAO YIN AND MEDITATION

Tao Yin, in itself, is a form of moving meditation. It supports all the Taoist meditative practices by activating the energy in the meridians and clearing the mind. When the body is weak and low in energy, it becomes quite difficult to meditate. Tao Yin supports the meditative process in a gentle and effective manner by freeing up blocked energy and relaxing the body.

Meditation trains one to sense, direct, and cultivate more energy. An important meditation practice in the Universal Tao system is the Microcosmic Orbit meditation. The Microcosmic Orbit is the circuit of energy that runs from the base of the spine to the head and down the middle of the torso to the perineum. This important energy circuit nourishes all the channels and meridians in the body. The Microcosmic Orbit meditation opens points on the palms, the soles of the feet, the mideyebrow, and the crown where energy can be absorbed, condensed, and transformed into new life force. Circulating energy within the Microcosmic Orbit removes blockages and activates more chi to revitalize the body. See my book *Taoist Cosmic Healing* for step-by-step instruction in this meditation.

Opening the Microcosmic Orbit dramatically increases the quantity of

Tao Yin and the Universal Tao System

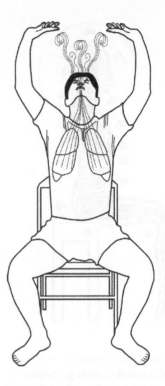

Activating the lungs in the Cosmic Healing Sounds meditation

our internal energy. The Tao Yin movements facilitate this opening. Through deep breathing and slow, powerful movements, the Tao Yin exercises bring forth an abundance of energy to use in opening the meridians.

It is recommended that you practice Tao Yin before meditation as a way to prepare yourself for the inner journey of meditation. After doing Tao Yin, meditation, or whatever else life offers during the day, it is especially beneficial to close the day by balancing the organs' energies with the Cosmic Healing Sounds meditation before going to bed. (My book *Taoist Cosmic Healing* details this practice as well.)

The Physical Benefits of Tao Yin

In the Universal Tao meditative exercises—Tai Chi, Iron Shirt Chi Kung, and Tao Yin—movement originates from the lower tan tien. This is the belly center of the body; it is considered to be the seat of awareness and is the home of the second brain. (The second brain will be discussed in greater depth in the next chapter.) With the Universal Tao practices one trains the awareness in the lower tan tien, coordinating all movements from the second brain. Movement from the tan tien extends out to the periphery of the body, to the arms and legs all the way to the tips of the fingers and the toes.

It is fairly easy to think of moving this way with our mind, but it is more difficult to actually move from the center consistently. The Tao Yin exercises are designed to help us find our center of gravity and to train us to move from our second brain. They strengthen the muscles involved in moving from the lower tan tien and enable us to actually move from that center in all the multiplanar possibilities.

Many people living in Western cultures have lost the natural flexibility of their bodies. People sit in chairs most of the day; they transport themselves by driving in cars (and thus sitting) instead of walking. As a culture we have lost our awareness of the center of the body and the importance of initiating movement from this area; when we do become aware of the low back it is usually because of pain that has developed from physical disuse or misuse. If we become aware of our abdominal area it is usually because it has lost its youthful flatness and has begun to demand a larger pants size.

The first step in regaining our strength and flexibility in the body's center is to become aware of the center in a new way. First, it is important to understand the actual structure of the area we call the tan tien. The pelvis, the base of the tan tien, is shaped like a bowl. When we are able to actually

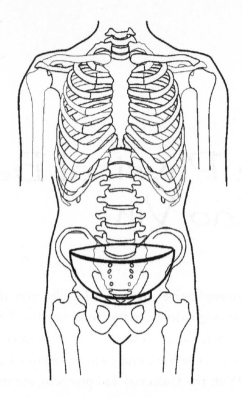

The "bowl" of the pelvis

rest the weight of the upper body into this bowl the whole structure of our body changes, as the weight we usually carry in our shoulders and upper body has a place to rest. Then the whole body begins to feel more at ease.

The pelvis is made up of a group of very strong bones. Several spaces, called foramen, allow for blood vessels, nerves, and muscles to pass from the lumbar area through the pelvis and to the legs. Attached to the bony structure of the pelvis are some of the strongest muscles in the body—the iliopsoas complex, the rectus femoris, the adductors, and the hamstrings. These muscles are all primary movers of the body.

THE PSOAS MUSCLE: THE BACK OF THE TAN TIEN

The iliopsoas complex is one of the most important muscles to access when learning to do Tao Yin, Iron Shirt Chi Kung I, or Tai Chi Chi Kung I. The psoas is a broad, flat muscle in the area of the low back. Like an octopus, it has branches extending out from both sides of the lower spinal vertebrae. It has two segments—psoas major and psoas minor; the psoas major is by far the larger of the two segments. The psoas major originates from the transverse processes of the twelfth thoracic vertebra (T12) and each of the five lumbar vertebrae (L1 to L5) and passes beneath the inguinal ligament in the groin area as it descends down the front surface of the ilium bones of the pelvis. It inserts into the lesser trochanter process on the inside front of the femur (the big bone in the upper leg). The smaller psoas minor segment shares the same origins as the psoas major but inserts into the sacroischial ligament. This ligament connects to the ischium tuberosity (at the back of the sitting bones).

In actual fact the psoas major is only the upper portion of the iliopsoas muscle. Another important component of the iliopsoas complex is the iliacus muscle. The iliacus is broadly attached to the upper front side of the ilium (the two big bones of the hip) and to the top of the sacrum. The iliacus portion of the iliopsoas complex joins the lower part of psoas major to merge as one muscle at about the level of the hip joint. The iliacus shares the same tendon attachment as the psoas major, attaching to the lesser trochanter of the femur, just below the hip joint. The joining of the iliacus with the psoas major is the reason the muscle is named the iliopsoas complex.

The psoas major can also be considered to have an indirect connection to the sacrum via the piriformis muscle. The piriformis connects to the sides of the front surface of the sacrum from the greater trochanter processes, located

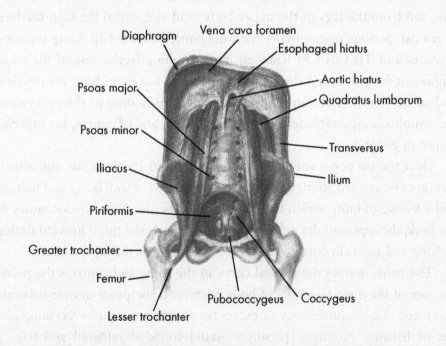

The iliopsoas complex. Notice how the iliacus joins the psoas major, merging into a common tendon that inserts at the lesser trochanter.

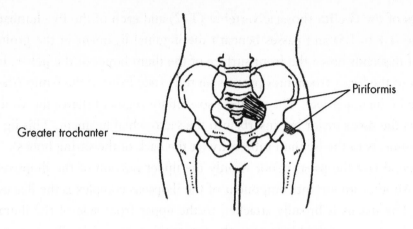

The piriformis muscle connects the greater trochanter to the sacrum.

at the back outsides of the femur bones near the hip joints. Since the psoas major connects to the lesser trochanter on the inside front of the femurs, a force exerted on one trochanter would affect the other. Several other muscles in the pelvic area have similar interrelationships with the psoas major.

The groin area in the front of the lower tan tien bowl, along with the sacrum/coccyx tilt of the lower spine, is the all-important *kua*. In Tai Chi movement, the transfer of force from the earth between the legs and the kua, and from the legs to the upper body (and vice versa) through the kua, is critical. Serious practitioners train diligently in both Chi Kung standing postures and Tai Chi Chi Kung to improve the effectiveness of their kua alignment for power and the smooth transfer of force (on both the physical and subtle levels). The Tao Yin training and conditioning of the psoas muscle complex is invaluable for developing the kua, and of course, for superior health in general.

Once the tan tien is energized and strengthened, the sensation and actualization of power and strength will create a sensation of well being and balance and a feeling of unity within the body. The psoas muscle is a major mover of the back, the hips, and the pelvis. The psoas propels the thigh forward during walking and assists in outward rotation of the thigh at the hip socket.

The psoas defines the natural curve in the spine and controls the pelvic tilt, one of the main elements of body posture. If the psoas muscle becomes shortened due to unnecessary or excess tension, this can pull everything else out of balance, causing a person to stand round-shouldered and have a slumped, swayback posture. A short psoas can also pull on the femur (thighbone), causing the leg to rotate outward. This torsion may prevent the foot

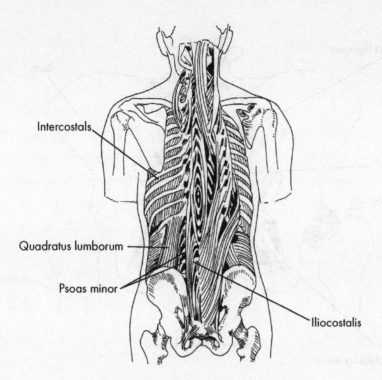

Intercostals

Quadratus lumborum

Psoas minor

Iliocostalis

The backside of the tan tien area

from resting squarely on the ground. The resulting foot roll during walking can create an additional source of stress and pain for the entire body.

The psoas can also be too short on just one side, causing many of the muscles on both sides of the body to compensate for the one-sided pull. This compensation can cause flat feet, bowlegged or knock-kneed alignments, weak ankles, cramping pain in the arches of the feet, tilting of the pelvis to one side, and pain and tenderness or stiffness of the spine. The pull of the psoas muscle can cause such rigidity that the thighbones will be unable to rotate properly and will cause grinding in the hip socket.

The two psoas major muscles form the main component of the iliopsoas complex that the Tao Yin exercises focus on. They are what is referred to when the simple term *psoas* is used.

As you can see, the psoas plays a critical role in maintaining balance for the structure of the body. This is one of the reasons why the Universal Tao exercises focus so intently on this area of the body. The greatest kinetic energy and power in the human body is generated through the hip joints, around which are attached the psoas muscles. If you cannot open the pelvic bowl (the iliac bones in the back) and learn to differentiate the two sides of the pelvis, the power of the hip joints is very limited. This lack of awareness

The Physical Benefits of Tao Yin

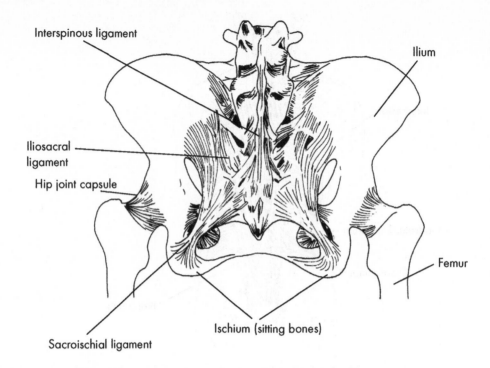

Back view of the kua and its bony and ligamentous components

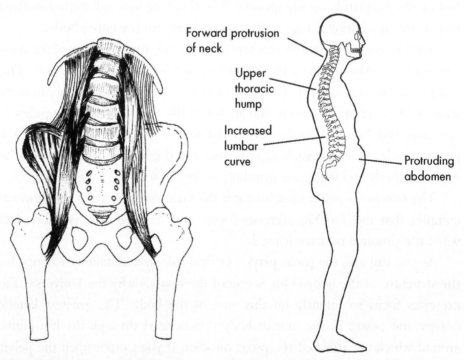

When the psoas is too short on one side, it pulls the spinal vertebrae of out alignment.

The physical effects of a misaligned psoas muscle

and movement also causes secondary loss of movement and therefore often causes pain in other parts of the body, along with a sense of weakness or powerlessness on the emotional level.

To put it simply, the iliopsoas complex provides the all-important connection through the pelvic area from the lower spine to the legs. As well, the psoas major has a critical relationship with the kidneys, heart, and thoracic diaphragm. "Seat of the Soul," "Soil of the Soul," and "Muscle of the Soul" are terms of respect accorded the psoas major muscle. These names give an indication of the vital impact the psoas has in relation to our structure, our organs, and the energetic state of our being. Of course, all of the other muscles, tendons, and ligaments in the psoas area are important, too. All benefit from the Tao Yin exercises.

THE KIDNEYS: PARTNER TO THE PSOAS

In addition to the vital importance of the psoas in the structural dynamics of the body, the psoas also plays a crucial role energetically. The psoas muscles support and hold the organs in the lower abdomen—in the tan tien bowl, home of the second brain. When it is relaxed and at its proper length, the psoas offers a supporting shelf for these organs. The psoas is especially

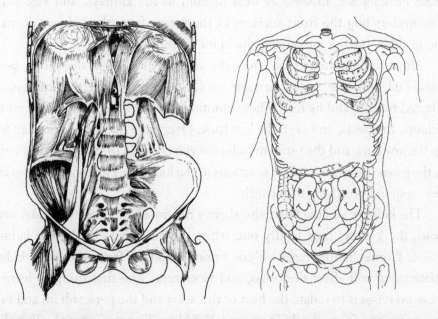

The kidneys and the psoas. The kidneys are positioned on the front side of each psoas muscle. The kidneys, psoas, and the lumbar region of the spine are warmed and energized by the Tao Yin exercises.

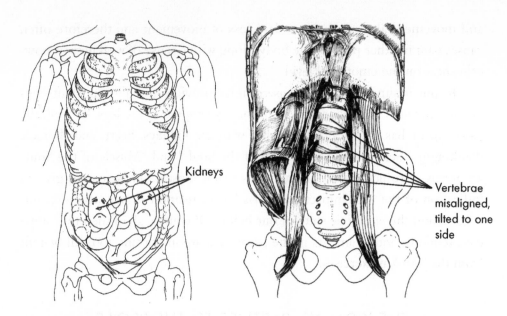

Kidney emotions affect the psoas. A cold or contracted psoas affects the kidneys and causes vertebral misalignment.

intimately related to the kidneys, since they are positioned directly on the front surface of the psoas muscle on each side of the spine. Along with the quadratus lumborum muscles, the psoas muscles form the back of the abdominal wall. Due to their direct physical contact with the kidneys, the psoas muscles are affected by heat or cold in the kidneys, and vice versa. The ureters hug the front surfaces of the psoas, from the kidneys down to the bladder, further enhancing the kidney energy connection.

All of the emotions that affect the kidneys also affect the psoas. Being associated with the water element in Chinese medicine, the kidneys are affected by cold and by fear. These emotions produce a chilling effect on the kidneys, the psoas, and even the low back. Over time these emotions can lock up the low back and the psoas muscle; conversely, cold or chronic contraction in the psoas can cause adverse reactions in the kidneys. The psoas and the kidneys respond positively to warmth.

The kidneys and the heart also share a relationship. When the heart overheats, the kidneys tend to dry out; when the heart is too cold, the kidneys freeze. Consequently, negative conditions resulting from the heart/kidney relationship will affect the psoas, and vice versa. The first thing to learn in these exercises is to sedate the heat of the heart and the pericardium and raise the water yin from the kidneys and Bubbling Springs upward. (Bubbling Springs is the Kidney 1 point at the bottom of each foot.) When the heart and the kidneys are balanced, the psoas will release.

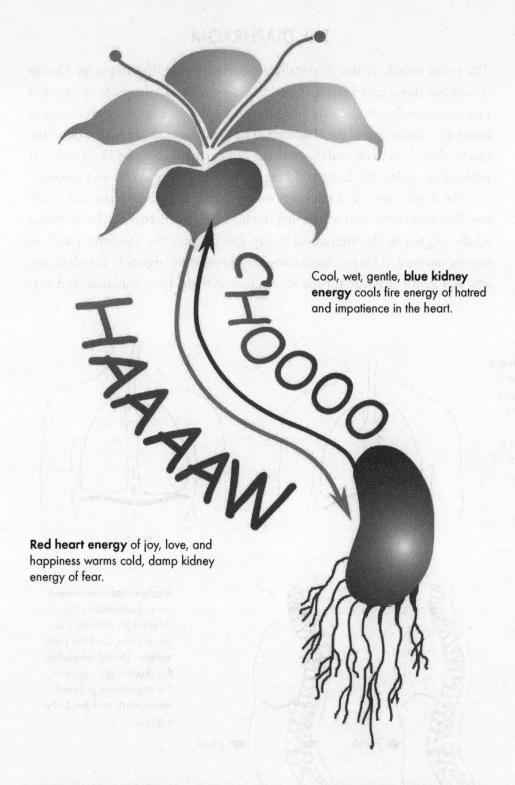

Cool, wet, gentle, **blue kidney energy** cools fire energy of hatred and impatience in the heart.

Red heart energy of joy, love, and happiness warms cold, damp kidney energy of fear.

Emotional energy balancing of heart and kidneys from the Cosmic Healing Sounds meditation. The subvocal organ sounds, "Cho-o-o-o-o" for the kidneys and "Haw-w-w-w-w" for the heart, are expressed during exhalation.

THE DIAPHRAGM

The psoas muscle is also physically connected to the diaphragm by fibrous connective tissue called fascia. The diaphragm is a wall of muscle and tendon that separates the chest cavity from the abdomen. It is the floor to the chest cavity and the ceiling to the abdomen. The diaphragm attaches all around the inside of the lower ribs and down to the lumbar spine. Shaped like a dome, it projects up against the heart and lungs, giving these organs lift and support.

The diaphragm is in a relaxed position during the exhale phase of breathing; the diaphragm contracts during the inhale phase, flattening down against all the organs in the abdominal cavity and causing the abdominal wall to expand outward. This rhythmic flattening against the organs in the abdomen acts as a gentle massage for the stomach, intestines, liver, pancreas, and kid-

Diaphragm movement. When the diaphragm is relaxed the dome rests against the heart and lungs. When the diaphragm contracts it pushes down against all of the organs in the abdominal cavity.

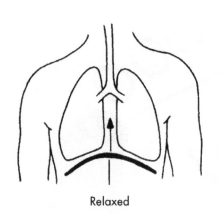

Relaxed

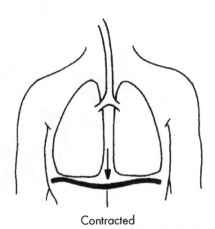

Contracted

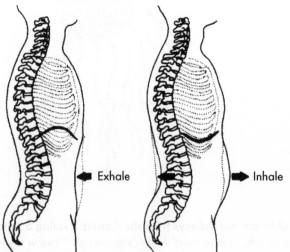

Exhale | Inhale

Abdominal movement. During exhalation the diaphragm relaxes, the organs rise, and the belly flattens. During inhalation the diaphragm contracts, the organs are pressed downward, and the belly expands.

neys. By lifting the heart and fanning the fires of digestion and metabolism, the diaphragm muscle plays a largely unheralded role in maintaining our health, vitality, and well being.

In the Empty Force training this breathing movement of the relaxed and contracted diaphragm and the expansion and contraction of the abdominal wall is developed further. By flattening the belly back toward the spine and holding the breath out, thereby moving trapped gas and stagnant chi in the abdomen, you create a vacuum and a resulting suction force. Holding the breath out and moving the diaphragm up and down gives the organs a powerful massage. The Empty Force Breath is also used to help direct the chi in Tao Yin movements. (See my book *Tan Tien Chi Kung* for more on Empty Force training.)

The diaphragm has one fascial sheet that reaches down and connects with the psoas. Muscle tightness or contraction in the low back will therefore affect the diaphragm, making it hard to breathe. If the psoas muscle is supple, one can breathe deeper and so utilize the power of the diaphragm to support movement and help connect the upper body with the lower body.

The diaphragm is sometimes known as the "spiritual muscle." Breathing brings in vital life energy, chi, that streams through the body. In this subtle inner sense, *breath* means "spirit"—and it is the link between the body and soul. Blockage of the breath is the beginning of most disease and illness in the body and the mind. Tao Yin exercises direct energy to relax the diaphragm, eliminate blockages, and restore a smooth flow of internal energy.

Breathing facilitates the flow of vital internal energy through the body; this process is an integral part of our health. Block this force, this energy of the breath, and we become ill. In Taoist practices this internal aspect of breathing—the primordial breath—is regarded as the most important element. This is what is called chi. In the Universal Tao, we often refer to this inner component of breath as *subtle breath* or *electric breath* to distinguish it from the outer aspect of breathing oxygen through the nose into the lungs. Tao Yin is the practice of breathing and moving this vital energy.

Stress and emotional conditioning can have profound effects on breathing. Breathing gets stuck and congested from stress. The diaphragm tightens and stiffens, and breathing becomes a matter of ribs moving up and down in fits and starts. The flowing rhythmic breath of a relaxed diaphragm is lost when we become seriously upset. Rest and relaxation will restore this rhythmic flow, but like the other muscles in our body, the diaphragm is eventually subject to taking on too much tension.

In the Tao, we say that the number one toxin in our bodies is negative emotions. We need to transform the unproductive negative emotions into positive and virtuous emotions. Tao Yin and the Inner Smile are ways to transform stress into energy and transform the negative to positive.

The major energy burned in the body is glucose, which comes from the carbohydrates we eat. An average Western diet consists of 70 percent carbohydrates, which break down into glucose; the by-product of that biochemical combustion is carbon dioxide, which we release through breathing. When we learn how to breathe properly, 70 percent of the toxins are expelled from our bodies. Unfortunately, however, most of us do not breathe properly. When we learn to breathe properly we release carbon dioxide to nature, to the plants and trees, which use our body toxins as nourishment and give us back oxygen.

THE TENDONS: FLEXIBILITY AND POWER

When we do not release the muscles and diaphragm and breathe fully, toxins accumulate in the joints, causing joint and muscle pain. When toxins accumulate the joints and tendons become stiff. Tao Yin focuses on the tendons, an often-overlooked part the body. When we think of the body's flexibility and power we tend to think of our muscles, but actually the tendons are a much more efficient source of power in our bodily movements. They provide us with a

A show of the flexibility and power of tendons.

dynamic flexibility, a potential to "spring back," like the quality we see in a slingshot or a bow and arrow. When we see a deer springing gracefully through the air, it is the dynamic flexibility and power of the tendons that we are admiring.

Tendons are found throughout the body, wherever the muscles connect to the skeleton. The tendons' role is to support the movement and structure of the body by connecting the muscles to the bones. Tendons are composed of fibrous connective tissue. The tissue is arranged in dense, regular bundles of fibers that give tremendous strength while still maintaining pliancy. Because of the special combination of strength and pliability, tendons have the unique capacity to absorb force or energy, hold that energy, and then discharge that energy into movement.

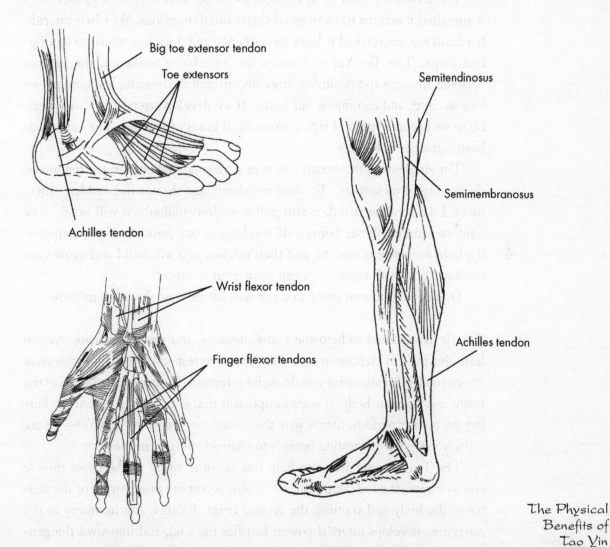

Tendons connect muscles to the bones throughout the body.

The Achilles tendon can absorb and hold up to two thousand pounds of force. All of the tendons work together to provide the body with a flexibility that is both powerful and dynamic. Like the dynamics of an antenna, the human body can be used as a structure to channel energy. The principle for this channeling is the same for psychic energies as for pure physical force. What keeps the skeletal structure intact and integrated are the tendons. Conditioning the tendons with Tao Yin exercises directly benefits the practice of Iron Shirt Chi Kung postures, which are taught as basic practices in the Universal Tao. The Iron Shirt postures help the student train the skeleton to be integrated and to channel physical force. Through this training one learns to channel chi, or psychic energies, as well.

The tendons should be as resilient as rubber bands. After a rubber band is stretched it returns to its original shape and dimensions. Yet when the rubber band is *over*stretched it loses its resiliency and does not return to its original shape. The Tao Yin exercises strive to achieve resiliency, the balance between strength and flexibility. If we overstretch the muscles and tendons we lose strength and can injure our joints. If we develop strength without flexibility we become stiff and rigid, prone to all kinds of injuries. The key to our health practice is balance.

The single most important factor in achieving resiliency in the tendons is the quality of movement. Tendons are elastic and do not like sudden movement. Like a rubber band, if you pull a tendon suddenly, it will break. The tendons cannot tolerate being held too long in one position: if you pull gently, hold for a few moments, and then release, you will build and grow your tendons. Yes, that's right—you can grow your tendons!

Do not rush. If you move in a soft and gentle way, the tendons grow.

Tao Yin is designed to help the joints, tendons, and muscles release. As you learn the Tao Yin exercises it is very important to rest and breathe into the areas where you feel tension after you do each movement. Eventually you will feel the toxins leaving your body. It is also important that you direct your energy during the resting periods; that is why these exercises are called Tao Yin—we are actively using the yin resting periods to channel energies in the body.

The Tao Yin exercises also help one become aware of the psoas muscle and to insure its good condition, while also becoming more aware of the center of the body and training the second brain. Balance and harmony in the psoas area develops internal power, fortifies the soul, and improves the general quality of our lives.

5

Tan Tien Consciousness: The Second Brain

In addition to its importance as the control center for the mechanics of the physical structure of the body, the lower tan tien also houses a treasure of even more far-reaching significance. Most of us who have had Taoist training in Chi Kung, Tai Chi, and various chi meditations and healing practices have often heard the reminder, "Be aware of your tan tien," but do most people really understand the meaning of this injunction to always be conscious of the tan tien? Probably not. Further, do we use our second brain as much as we can? I think definitely not.

Throughout the world there are institutions to train the brain in the head, and that's good. But what about training the "second brain" in the abdominal area? I had never before thought of second-brain development in terms of "training," even though that's exactly what I've been doing all of my life in my Taoist studies. But about ten years ago, through my participation in several brain-wave studies, I came to understand a few simple concepts that are important to Universal Tao, and I want to share those revelations with you. It started in 1994, when Dr. Rhonda Jessum, a clinical psychologist in Los Angeles, asked me to undergo some brain-wave testing. I agreed. The machines at that time didn't tell us much, but it was discovered that when I did the Cosmic Inner Smile meditation, my brain waves slowed down dramatically, while at the same time my beta waves increased to a very high level. In other words, my higher functions were such that I could drive a car, but my brain was at what was considered a resting and sleeping stage. The puzzled researchers asked, "Hey, how did you do that?" At that time, I didn't know.

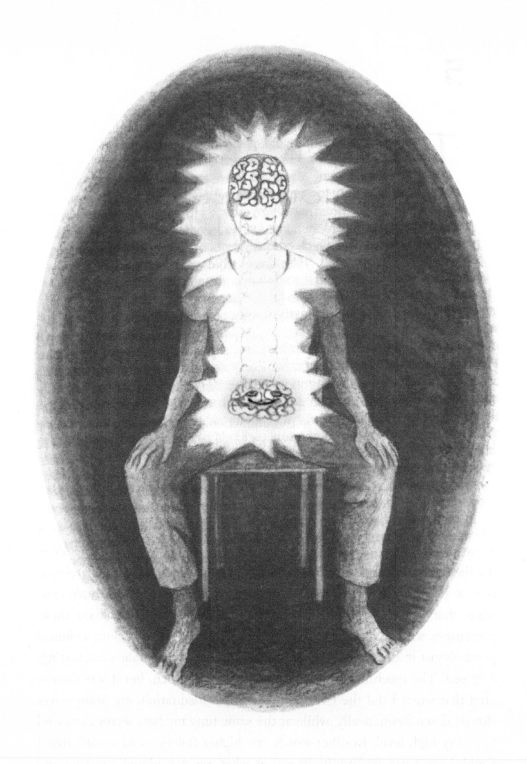

The second brain in the tan tien

After that, I was invited to start testing with the Institute for Applied Biocybernetics and Feedback Research in Vienna, one of the biggest institutes for training top athletes in Europe. Researchers there have developed an instrument that can measure the brain's potential energy, which represents all the energy in the body. The researchers said that their findings prove to the West that chi exists, that there is energy and a life force running in the body. Their instrument also determines how much energy a person has for the whole day and how much of that energy is for mental clarity and body power.

With the researchers watching and measuring, I did the Cosmic Inner Smile, smiling into my abdomen. They picked up the brain-wave readings quickly and said, "Your brain waves are going lower, lower, and resting—and you are nearly in the sleeping state." At the same time, my muscle tension, heart rate, and skin resistance were all very low. Then I surged the energy up from my abdomen to my brain, and the researchers started to see that the energy actually charged up there. They were quite amazed and said, "Hey, this is what we're looking for!"

They asked me what I was doing, and I said, "I'm smiling to my abdomen." They kept on talking to me and asking me questions. They discovered that my observing brain (my head-brain) was not very active; it was still in a very light resting state. But then how could I answer their questions? They said, "Hey, look! Master Chia is talking to us in his sleep. How can he talk to us in his sleep?"

At last I began to understand. A constant injunction of Taoist practice is "Train the second brain in order to use the second brain." The first (observing) brain and the second (feeling and awareness) brain are linked, and both can carry our consciousness. The second brain charges the observing brain with energy, either purposefully, such as when I surged energy from my lower tan tien up to the upper tan tien, or by default, when by having consciousness in the second brain we allow the first brain to rest. Perhaps it will be easier to understand the first brain and second brain relationship if we call the first brain the "logical" brain and the second brain the "intuitive" brain. The gut, or intuitive brain, receives important messages about our bodies and the world outside and passes these messages to our logical brain. When we strive to listen effectively to our intuitive brain with our logical brain, the result is a better connection to ourselves.

The existence of the feeling and awareness brain has since been proven. In 1996 an article about the "hidden brain in the gut" was published in the *New York Times*. It described the work of researchers who had found that the gut, the enteric nervous system, functioned similarly to the brain. They had discovered that the large and small intestines had the same type of neurons as are found in the brain and that the gut can send and receive impulses, record experiences, and respond to emotions. In other words, the gut functioned very much like a brain. Soon after, a book on the subject, called *The Second Brain*, was published.

The *Times* article posed the question, "Can the gut learn?" A Taoist would respond with an emphatic yes. Almost five thousand years of Tao practice has taught us that we must train all the organs to do different things. In this way, we can use the gut as our conscious brain and allow the head brain to rest. Why is this important? Because the head brain is a "monkey mind," riddled with doubt, shame, guilt, and suspicion. It is always thinking, planning, or worrying. Most people just think and think and think. Scientists have discovered that when people spend a lot of time worrying, their upper (in the head) brain uses a lot of energy. They say that the upper brain can use up to 80 percent of the body's energy, leaving only 20 percent for the organs.

We need to use the brain in the head in order to perform complex functions such as reasoning, making plans, and making calculations. These are typical left-brain functions. However, for our daily life of consciousness, awareness, and feeling, which is typically governed by the right brain, we can use either the brain in the head or the brain in the gut. When we use the upper brain less, it becomes charged with energy and its power increases, and as a result more power is available to the body. When the upper brain is resting, brain repair and maintenance occur and new brain cells can grow. This is the reason Taoism insists that we train the feeling and awareness brain in the gut—so that we can use it when the upper brain is resting. With more charging of the upper brain, we have more power for creativity or whatever we want to use it for. If we like, we can use it to develop our higher spiritual nature.

Consider it this way: For the same job, the head brain charges you eighty dollars, while the gut brain charges you only twenty dollars. So which one do you use? We are not silly enough to choose the overpriced package when we can have the same quality work done for less cost. But in terms of our own conscious life, we don't know how to choose the more cost-efficient package. We always use the high-priced upper brain. Even worse, we continue using it and using it, until the brain energy is completely consumed. At a certain point, the brain—and concurrently, the body and spirit—becomes empty of energy.

Whenever I smile down, the brain waves in my upper brain decrease very quickly, and the transformed energy from the lower tan tien and organs

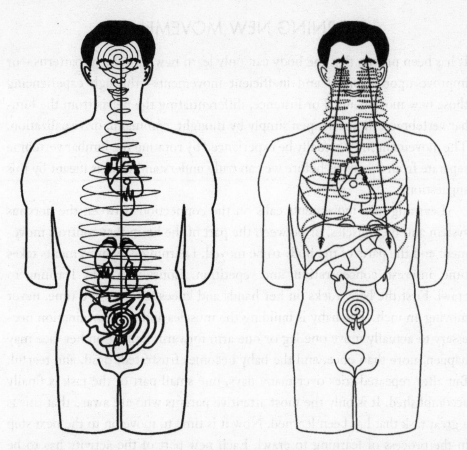

Chi transformation in Wisdom Chi Kung. In the Wisdom Chi Kung practice, the chi transformed in the heart and small intestines charges upward to fill the front center of the brain. When the mind is empty, transformed energy from all of the organs can charge the brain with chi.

charges the upper brain. By just flexing the facial muscles into the position of a genuine smile, we can produce the same effects on the nervous system that normally go with a natural spontaneous smile. We can actually make ourselves relaxed and happy by taking advantage of this built-in human mechanism. It's nautral. Just do it! Learning to smile down to the abdominal area and maintain an awareness of the relaxed, smiling sensation in the lower tan tien is the first step in training the second brain.

Remember these rules:

1. *Empty your mind down to the lower tan tien, and fill the lower tan tien with chi.* Where the mind goes, the chi flows.
2. *When your mind is empty, it will be filled.* When the organs have extra energy, that extra energy will rise up and fill the brain with chi.

Tan Tien
Consciousness:
The Second
Brain

41

LEARNING NEW MOVEMENTS

It has been proven that the body can only learn new movement patterns—or improve upon habitual and inefficient movements—through experiencing those new movements. For instance, differentiating the pelvis from the lumbar vertebrae will not happen simply by thought, command, or visualization. The movement must actually be experienced by rotating the lumbar vertebrae separate from the pelvis before we can truly understand what is meant by this suggestion.

Learning new movements calls on the connection between the nervous system and the muscles, or between the part of the brain that controls movement and the parts of the body to be moved. Learning new movements takes time, interest, concentration, and repetition. Consider a baby learning to crawl. First the baby rocks on her hands and knees for days at a time, never moving an inch. The baby is building the muscles and the coordination necessary to actually move one leg or one arm forward. Falling on her face may happen more than once, and the baby becomes frustrated, tired, and tearful. But after repeated tries over many days, one small part of the task is finally accomplished. It is only the most attentive parents who are aware that this is a great task that has been learned. Now it is time to move on to the next step in the process of learning to crawl. Each new part of the activity has to be learned increment by increment, as each part is essential to the totality of the movement.

In learning to alter our movement, it helps to remember the patience and persistence of the baby, who intuitively approaches each new activity in small steps. To move the lumbar vertebrae without moving our neck or shoulders requires a similar kind of systematic, cumulative learning. We must be able to sense where the lumbar vertebrae are in our body and to discover the movements possible there. Take a moment to touch the lumbar area of your spine with your hands. Feel each bony spinous process with your fingers. Find the spaces between the vertebrae. Notice the shapes and sensations in your body as you explore this area. Begin to move this part of your spine around while still holding your hand there and see if you can move the lumbar area separately from the rest of your spine. Bring all of your awareness and attention to this part of your body. Concentrate on moving the lumbars without moving any other part of your spine.

Begin to experiment with the movements possible in your lumbar area. Can you move one vertebra separately from the rest? Can you move one vertebra forward, toward your navel? Can you move one vertebra back? The

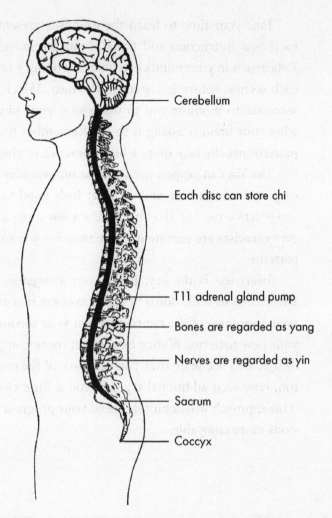

The human spine. The bones of the spinal column contain the highest concentration of marrow in the body. The junctions between the vertebrae store chi. The nerves of the spinal cord provide a pathway for earth and sexual energies to move up to the head.

Cerebellum

Each disc can store chi

T11 adrenal gland pump

Bones are regarded as yang

Nerves are regarded as yin

Sacrum

Coccyx

movement of a part of your body that you have not focused on before is sometimes frustrating and uncomfortable. See what emotions arise as you focus on twisting just your lumbar area to the left or right without moving your shoulders or your head along with it.

There are good reasons why we have the impulse to initiate the movement of the spine from our shoulders or head. The human nervous system is set up to turn the body where the eyes lead us so that we can see where we are going. So if we want to move the lumbar region first, we must teach our nervous system to behave differently. Such repatterning can only occur through slow, gentle, repetitive movements, because it is the limbic part of the brain that must learn the movement first. That "hind brain," as it is sometimes called, is very complicated and relatively slow to learn new movements. However, as you gradually train the neurons of the limbic brain by repeating simple new movements, you will find that the activity becomes progressively easier.

Take your time to learn the exercises presented in this book. Stop with each new instruction and think about the movement you are about to do. Rehearse it in your mind's eye first. Try doing a little at a time and really learn each section before going on to the next. Watch yourself in a mirror or ask someone to monitor you to make sure your physical body is indeed doing what your brain is asking it to do. Remember that old, ingrained movement patterns usually take quite a bit of practice to change.

Tao Yin can be practiced a little bit everyday or every other day. Take it easy in the beginning and do what feels good to your body. Eventually you can practice the full Tao Yin routine a few times a week, or you can use whatever exercises are pertinent at the time for you to learn these new movement patterns.

Awareness is the key. Bring your awareness fully into each movement. Remember to smile down to your lower tan tien and keep it relaxed. Maintain your awareness of the tan tien so that your second brain also feels and learns your new patterns. Notice how much more complete your kinesthetic sense of that area becomes after you've repeated the exercise several times. Notice, too, how each additional try gets you a little closer to achieving your goal. This approach will definitely speed your progress and make your Tao Yin sessions more enjoyable.

6

Preparation and General Instructions

Start by preparing the area where you will practice. It's advisable to use a quiet place and take the phone off the hook so you will not be disturbed. The temperature should be comfortable and the lighting soft and gentle on your eyes. If available, use a large mirror to monitor your positions and progress. Arrange an exercise mat, a slightly cushioned pad, or a folded blanket on the floor, giving yourself enough space to spread out easily. Your bed or a firm but soft carpet can serve as well. The point is to make things as comfortable as possible on a firm base so that during the exercises you can relax and enjoy yourself more fully.

Set aside a convenient time when you can really get away from things. Make it a special time in your day devoted to yourself. Plan to spend sixty minutes for each session. Many people find it best to do Tao Yin exercises first thing in the morning. This is an excellent way to start your day. Another good time is in the evening, an hour or two after a light supper. Whenever you practice, leave at least an hour after any meal before you exercise. Before you begin, be sure to empty your bladder and bowels if necessary. Your clothing should be loose and comfortable. Remove your shoes and socks before starting.

The Tao Yin exercises in this book are divided into five sets of movements. They start with basic breathing and progress through an emphasis on key parts of the body. Each set contains a series of exercises, each of which builds on the previous one. It's best to learn the exercises in the order presented. After learning the sets in chapters 7 and 8, you may want to alternate some of the exercises on different days as you progress through the remaining chapters. The learning phase takes time. You can formulate your own practice strategy as you gain experience. Eventually, you will be sufficiently proficient to go through all five sets in about an hour. Together, they open and energize the entire body.

The most important aspect of the Tao Yin practice is to enjoy yourself. Keep this in mind as you practice: *Smile to yourself, to your second brain in your tan tien, and to the parts of the body you are moving.*

General Instructions

- **Smile:** Before, during, and after your practice, smile. The Universal Tao recognizes the influence of the deep facial muscles that reflect our true, loving smile. The pituitary gland responds to the movement of our "loving smile" muscles, switching on the parasympathetic nervous system (the relaxation response), transforming stress into vital energy in the process.

- **Empty the mind down:** With the smiling sensation gleaming in the mind and enlivening the face, beam the smiling mind down to the second brain in the tan tien.

- **Breathe with the tan tien:** In tan tien breathing the abdomen rises and falls in a sympathetic movement with the "spiritual muscle," the diaphragm.

- **Rest between movements:** All of the exercises have an active moving phase and a passive observing phase—a yang phase and a yin phase. Pause and rest between movements. The yin phase allows the immediate benefits of the exercise to be acknowledged by the mind and absorbed by the still, resting body. Physical and emotional tensions are relaxed, toxins are released, and chi heals and refreshes as the smiling golden energizing light is directed to the area of focus.

- **Do full-body tan tien breathing sometimes:** Breathe from the crown of the head to the bottom of the heels, balancing hot and cold, during rest.

- **Do the Lotus Meditation sometimes:** Meditate on the lotus and on the harmonious equilibrium of the kidneys' water energy and the heart's fire energy during rest.

- **Lead from the tan tien:** Lead most movements from the back of the lower tan tien in the lumbar region of the back. Don't lead with the head. Tuck the chin lightly to lock the neck, inducing the head to follow.

- **Be gentle and flexible:** When stretching your body, feel the stretch, but don't go too far. It is not helpful to cram or pull your body into these positions. Respond to pain by easing up until you return to your comfort zone. Relax and open your body to go deeper into the positions. Create strength and power through subtle internal work on your structure. "Not too much, not too little. Ah-h-h! That's the Tao!"

- **Breathe in golden energizing light:** During rest, breathe golden energizing light and breathe out cloudy gray tired, stale, sick energy. The energy follows our attention; therefore, we smile into those special areas of the body that the exercise works. For example, smile to the psoas and the golden light energy flows to the psoas.
- **Study each new exercise:** Before attempting a new Tao Yin exercise, read through the exercise from the first word to the last and study the illustrations.
- **Enjoy!**

The Tao Yin exercises always begin with the breath. Working with the breath is an integral part of the practice. The breath is a reliable guide for moving deeper into the body and deeper into a stretch. The breath is a bridge that connects the body with the mind and the mind with the spirit. Tao Yin is meditation in motion, integrating all of our separate parts into wholeness.

The control and coordination center in the body for smoothly integrating all of these bodily activities is the second brain in the lower tan tien. Training this visceral brain—our "gut brain," which can feel and can achieve a high level of awareness—is a pleasant and very important part of Tao Yin practice.

1. First, bring the smiling sensation into the face, letting go of tension in the forehead and jaws, and bring softness to the skin throughout the face.
2. Direct this relaxed smile down to the heart and bring in thoughts of love, joy, and happiness. Empty the mind and heart down to the lower tan tien (the abdomen, from the navel down) to near the top of the pubic bone.
3. Keep the smiling sensation in the lower tan tien and keep checking yourself to make sure that you maintain the relaxed smiling awareness there. This will help to coordinate the breath with the correct performance of the exercises.

Only when the breath is experienced as a fullness through the whole body do we begin the stretches.

導引
Tao Yin

PART 2

Tao Yin Exercises

Set 1
Foundations—Conscious Breathing, Energy Balancing, Spine and Psoas Conditioning

The practices learned in this chapter serve as a foundation to build upon in learning the movements in succeeding chapters. The first exercise, Full-Body Breathing, relaxes and calms the body so that you can gain more benefits from doing the other exercises. Full-Body Breathing helps you develop the skills of conscious breathing, breathing with healing golden light, and learning to direct the subtle, electric breath throughout the body, a most important aspect of the Tao Yin practice that takes place during the passive resting phase between physical exertions and movements. All of the exercises in set 1 begin in the supine (lying on the back) position (fig. 1.1).

In this set of exercises special attention is given to conditioning and retraining the spine and the psoas muscle—vital to the structure of the whole body. Energetically, you begin to balance the fire and water energies of the heart and kidneys, which has a dramatic impact on the psoas muscle (and vice versa). This energy balancing is accomplished through the combination of exercises, breathing, and meditation.

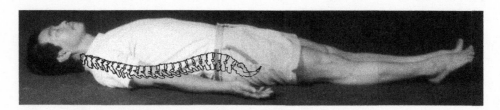

Fig. 1.1 Beginning position: Lying on back with normal spinal curvature

Exercises in This Set

1. Full-Body Breathing
2. River Flows into the Valley
3. Water Up and Fire Down
4. Lotus Meditation
5. Monkey Rests with Knees in Air
6. Crocodile Lifts Head
7. Monkey Clasps Knees
8. Monkey Pushes against Knees
9. Monkey Prays with Elbows
10. Monkey Prays Counterpose: Clasp Knees
11. Twist Body Like a Snake
12. Monkey Flaps Legs

 Full-Body Breathing

We begin this set with the breath because all of the exercises in this book work with the combination of breath, movement, and flexibility. In general, every movement begins with an exhale and every resting period begins with an inhale. Be conscious of your breathing throughout your practice. Remind yourself to gently close your lips and to breathe in and out through the nose.

Normal, or "regular," breathing has no colors associated with it. If you go to the forest and breathe this way, you take in "unleaded regular," a step up from city air but not the best that nature has to offer. As you learn how to inhale golden light, you begin to add "super octane" fuel to your system. Smile to your lungs and visualize that you are connecting with smiling golden sunshine as you inhale, then draw the golden light into your body with your breath. This process helps to integrate the mind with the body.

When you exhale, visualize a cloudy gray color leaving the body. Be aware of your lungs and feel as though you are releasing all of the air from your lungs without tension. Visualize your lungs getting smaller and smaller.

When done regularly and correctly, this kind of breathing works to develop the psoas, diaphragm, and abdominal muscles in a balanced way. Breathing in the golden color, you take in healing energy; as you exhale the cloudy gray color, you expel toxins and carbon dioxide. This is a very efficient way to release these substances. The relaxation allows you to release those toxins. When you are tense, the toxins stagnate in your muscles and joints.

1. **Hands on navel:** Lie comfortably on your back, face up, legs extended and slightly apart. Place your hands on your navel, the right hand on top of the left (fig. 1.2). Feel the weight of the palms resting on the belly. Take a few very deep breaths and relax. Smile down to your organs and your second brain. As you inhale, expand the lower abdomen. Exhale in a comfortable way, letting the abdomen relax. As you exhale, let any negative energy flow out with your breath, imagining it to be a cloudy gray color.

   Continue with your breathing: inhale, expanding the abdomen and the navel area, then exhale the toxins in your body and relax. Exhaling a cloudy, gray color is a way to help eliminate toxins. When you inhale, breathe in golden light, the "super octane" energy. Gradually extend the subtle breath so that the golden energy gathers in the area of your focused attention, behind the navel area under the hands.

   Continue breathing in this way for a minute or so. Feel the golden light sink deeper with successive breaths. As you progress in your practice, you will sense this subtle breath very clearly.

2. **Hands on lower abdomen:** Move your palms down to the lower abdomen and separate your hands: right palm on right side, left palm on left side (fig. 1.3). Inhale, feeling the lower abdomen expand; exhale the cloudy gray color, releasing any sickness or suppressed emotions. Inhale, visualizing golden light entering your body as you fill the lower abdomen with energy. Continue breathing with your palms and your attention on the lower abdomen for about two minutes.

3. **Hands on upper abdomen:** Cover the upper abdomen with your palms above the navel and below the rib cage (fig. 1.4). Take long, slow breaths, sinking the golden light deeply into the body. Exhale out the cloudy, gray substances. Feel calm and peaceful.

   Comment: These first three steps, sometimes called tan tien breathing, are good to do anytime you feel tired or depleted. The breathing helps reduce tension and release toxins. Spend about ten minutes doing this tan tien breathing and you will feel refreshed. The complete sequence of Full-Body Breathing that follows is very beneficial, especially as a prelude to your Tao Yin practice.

   This conscious breathing is a much healthier habit than drinking a cup of coffee or smoking a cigarette! Caffeine and nicotine stimulate the adrenal glands, making you temporarily alert. However, the benefits of these substances are short term and deplete your adrenal energy. The harmful effects of adrenal depletion become cumulative, leading to weakened kidneys and a weakened constitution and immune system. Slow and conscious breathing will energize and benefit your body for your entire life.

4. **Hands on groin area:** Put your palms on the groin area, inside the hips: right hand on right side and left hand on left side. Spread your legs shoulder-width apart. Be aware of the groin area and breathe to it. Eventually you will feel the expansion and contraction of the groin. Release any tension you might be holding here. Tension can accumulate as a result of suppressed sexual feelings or sexual tension or dissatisfaction. By breathing into this area we allow it to open in an effective and

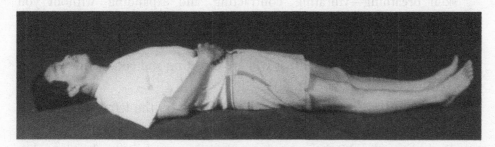

Fig. 1.2 Place your hands on your navel, the right hand on top of the left.

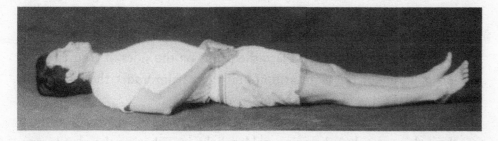

Fig. 1.3 Continue breathing with your palms covering each side of the lower abdomen.

Fig. 1.4 Palms are above the navel and below the rib cage.

natural way. This simple breathing is very powerful. Feel the energy begin to release in the sexual area and in the groin area. Let the tension release as a cloudy gray color with each exhalation. Feel that you are exhaling down through the legs and out through the soles of the feet and the toes. Inhale golden light. Continue breathing in this way for two minutes.

5. **Hands on sacrum and base of skull:** Bend your right knee, placing your right foot flat on the floor. Rotate your lower body to the left so you can comfortably put your right palm on your sacrum (your tailbone); place your left palm at the base of your skull (fig. 1.5). Inhale fully and slowly, bringing the golden light into the whole spine. Exhale, gently squeezing out any cloudy gray color. Gradually feel the sacrum and the base of the skull breathing—vibrating, contracting, and expanding, without you doing anything. Just by directing the breath in this way you will eventually begin to feel the movement and the release of tension in these places. These sensations indicate that you are directing and conducting chi—an essential aspect of Tao Yin.

6. **Hands on lower ribs:** Place your right palm on the left lower ribs and the left palm on your right lower ribs, crossing your arms and letting the diaphragm relax. Notice any pain or tension as you breathe. It's normal to feel some tension as you release blockages. Feel the diaphragm moving up and down, the lungs moving up and down, the ribs moving in and out. Continue breathing with attention in your lower ribs.

7. **Hands on middle chest:** Move your hands up to the middle of your chest, crossing your arms. Place the palms on the sides of your ribs, the left palm under the right armpit and right palm under the left armpit (fig. 1.6). Feel your lungs expanding on the inhale.

    Now as you inhale and exhale, imagine that you are also breathing through your palms, bringing golden light in, ushering the cloudy gray color out. Many people have problems breathing into this area because of emotional suppression, which can block the upper lungs and congest the chest. Inhale, feeling your palms on your ribs. Exhale the emotional tension out as a cloudy gray color. Inhale and extend your chest toward your palms. Exhale, gently squeezing your lungs smaller and smaller. Inhale and exhale with full attention on your breathing. Continue breathing in this way for two minutes.

8. **Hands on upper ribs:** Move your hands upward to gently cover the upper ribs, below the clavicles (the collarbones). Your right palm cov-

ers the right side, the left palm covers the left side (fig. 1.7). Breathe. Feel your upper lungs expand with the incoming breath. Inhale the golden light fully into your upper lungs. Exhale out the gray, cloudy toxins, feeling the breath move your ribs as you inhale and exhale effortlessly.

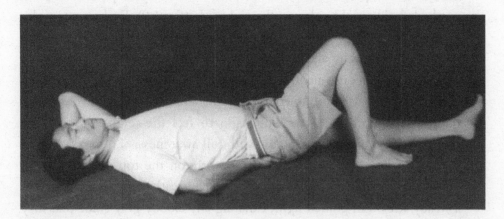

Fig. 1.5 Place your left palm on the base of your skull and your right palm on your sacrum (tailbone).

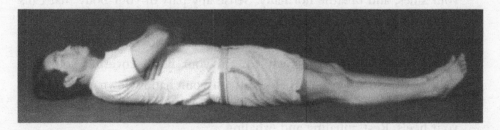

Fig. 1.6 Place your palms on the sides of your ribs, the left palm under the right armpit and right palm under the left armpit.

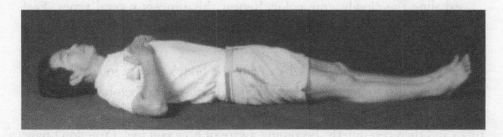

Fig. 1.7 Place the palms on the upper ribs, under the clavicles.

9. **Hands on sides of neck:** Cover both sides of the neck gently with your palms: right palm on the left side, left palm on the right side (fig. 1.8). Feel the neck expanding and contracting. Be soft, flexible, and gentle. Breathe naturally. When you breathe well you feel the energy, the chi, moving from the bottom of your body to the top. Feel the subtle expansion and contraction of your neck as you breathe for a few minutes in this manner.

10. **Hands on temples:** Cover your temple bones with your palms: left palm on the left side, right palm on the right side (fig. 1.9). Feel your temples breathe. Don't worry if it is difficult to sense this movement right away, just breathe naturally and soon you will feel them lightly expanding and contracting. Don't use any force—just let the sense of movement come to you. With close attention to your breathing and the contact of your hands on your temple bones, you will begin to feel the temples move very slightly with your breath. Breathe with full awareness.

11. **Hands on crown:** Place both hands gently on the top of your crown, sensing expansion and contraction with each breath (fig. 1.10). Breathe in a steady stream of golden light, exhaling any cloudy gray color that may be left in your body. Bring total awareness to every breath as you feel your crown breathing.

12. **Balancing—not too hot, not too cold:** Now relax, put your hands to your sides, and breathe normally. Sense any part of your body that calls for your attention and breathe, smiling golden light into that area.

Direct the chi from your head down to the soles of your feet. Inhale, raising your hands very slowly toward your head, covering your face lightly with soft hands. Exhale and rub your hands down your throat, down your chest, down to your groin, and let the energy move down to your heels. Rest, inhaling and exhaling.

Now very slowly bring your hands up, bringing the chi into you. Again exhale and rub your hands down your face, down your neck and chest. Very slowly guide the chi to your groin, then to your heels and out, exhaling the cloudy gray color. Repeat this process several times. Feel your energy cooling, all the way down to your feet.

The Tao is concerned with balancing the body's energy so that it is neither too hot nor too cold. This is a good exercise to do before settling into bed for a relaxed and deep, restful sleep. Repeat this energy balancing several times and then rest quietly, becoming aware of how you feel. (You don't have to do all of this breathing at once. You can break it up into segments.)

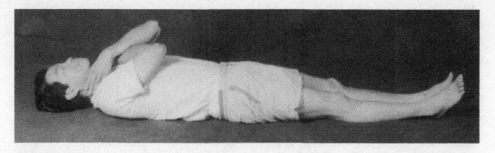

Fig. 1.8 Cover both sides of the neck with your palms: right side with the left palm, left side with the right palm.

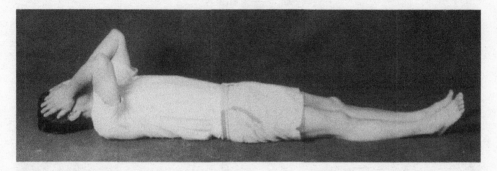

Fig. 1.9 Place the palms on your temple bones.

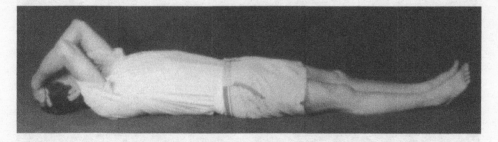

Fig. 1.10 Place both hands gently on the top of the crown, sensing expansion and contraction.

The effects of conscious chi breathing can be likened to breaking through ice, the "ice" being the frozen areas in the body. As the subtle chi breath sinks deeper into the body, these tension areas begin to melt. With time, like ice in the warm sun, the "frozen" tense and toxic areas areas transform from ice into water and then from water into chi "gas," evaporating in the form of cloudy gray energy.

Set 1:
Foundations

Golden River and Valley. In the River Flows into the Valley exercise, the energizing golden light flows down "the riverbed" formed by the raised thoracic vertebrae of the spine into the "valley" created by the lumbar tilt. The conscious breathing process described in Full-Body Breathing is used during the Tao Yin exercises. Golden life-giving energy is drawn in with the breath and, during the resting phase, cloudy gray energy of released toxins and tensions flows down into Mother Earth, where it is transformed. The energy is recycled up through the plants to help maintain a healthy balance in nature.

River Flows into the Valley
Meridian activated: Bladder (yang)

1. **Lie on back, bend knees, slide feet toward body.** Lying on your back, slide both feet up toward your buttocks, feet flat on the floor and knees up (fig. 1.11). This position releases the sacrum and the lumbar spine toward the floor. Breathe deeply.

2. **Exhale, press lumbar spine to mat, tilt pelvis.** On an exhale, tuck your chin in toward your chest and press your five lumbar vertebrae toward the mat, tilting your pelvis to gently lift your sacrum. Raise your chest from the lower thoracic vertebrae, letting the head follow in the arc of the crescent curve created in the upper spine (fig. 1.12).

   Comment: The purpose of this controlled movement is to activate the psoas muscle. When you raise your upper body slightly, you activate the psoas, not the abdominal muscles. That is the purpose of this movement.

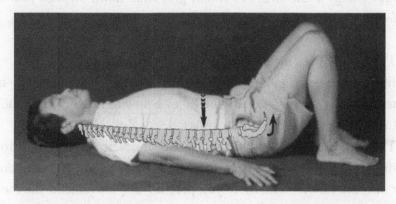

Fig. 1.11 Beginning position

Fig. 1.12 Raised position: The simultaneous lifting of the sacrum and the thoracic vertebrae as you press the lumbar vertebrae to the mat creates the valley.

Set 1:
Foundations

59

The head only follows in this movement. If you bring your head up too far, you will contract the abdominal muscles and you will not be able to breathe well.

3. **Inhale and release.** Inhale as you gently release your lumbar vertebrae. Let your sacrum return to the mat first, then one by one return the thoracic vertebrae to the mat. Totally relax your spine and psoas.

4. **Rest and smile, then repeat.** Rest now and smile to the whole spine. The resting period is very important. Feel a stream of chi flow from the head down the spine to the lumbar vertebrae, the psoas, and to the sacrum/coccyx. Repeat this movement three to six times.

5. **Straighten legs and rest.** When you have completed your repetitions, straighten your legs along the mat and take a longer rest. Breathe to the areas affected by the movement, especially the lumbar spine and the psoas muscle. Smile to those areas and feel fully relaxed, drawing the smiling golden energizing light to the area with your in-breath. Exhale any tensions, toxins, and tired energy in the form of a cloudy gray color down through your legs and feet into a hole in the ground, to be transformed by Mother Earth.

The River Flows into the Valley exercise is aptly named. The simultaneous lifting of the sacrum and the thoracic vertebrae as you press the lumbars to the mat while exhaling creates the valley below the abdomen, in the area of the five lumbar vertebrae and the psoas.

The raised upper body—the twelve thoracic vertebrae—forms the riverbed. Thus, the golden energizing light flows from the head "down the river into the valley." The more you practice this movement, the more profound your realization of the river and valley and the energetic flow becomes. Practice a little every day.

This movement is fundamental to this first set of Tao Yin exercises. Get this one and you will easily achieve results in the other exercises.

 ## Water Up and Fire Down

Meridians activated: Kidney and Pericardium (Lao Gong Point) (yin); Bladder and Stomach (yang)

In Tao Yin it's important to bring the excess heat from the heart down to the psoas muscle and the kidneys. This relaxes and warms the psoas muscle and the lower back. From the Bubbling Springs (Kidney 1) point on the sole of each foot, you can raise the water energy up to the kidneys and to the heart to nourish fire or to cool excess heat. The psoas doesn't like cold. When the muscle is cold, the muscle will contract and pull the spine toward the thigh. Cold and fear from the kidneys can affect the psoas, causing it to contract and thereby impacting negatively on the body's condition. The two-part exercise Water Up and Fire Down balances the fire and water elements in the body, creating harmony throughout the entire system.

☯ Activating the Bubbling Springs

1. **Inhale—flex toes:** Lie on your back, legs extended and slightly apart, arms at your sides. As you inhale, gently flex your toes back toward your head (fig. 1.13); feel the soles of your feet stretch open. Feel suction drawing water energy up into your soles. Do this until you feel moderate tension in your calves.

2. **Hold—feel chi from feet:** Feel bubbling chi rising up from the Bubbling Spring points to your kidneys and upward, pouring into your heart.

3. **Exhale—lumbars to mat, heart to psoas:** As you exhale, relax your feet and your chest. Feel the heart sink down toward the spine as you lightly press your lumbar spine toward the mat. Feel excess heat from your pericardium and your heart flowing down through your spine to the psoas muscle and the kidneys, warming them up. The psoas will feel relaxed and expanded and fear will melt away from the kidneys.

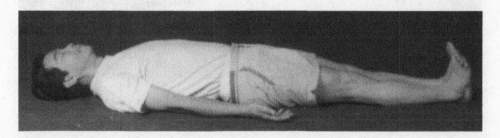

Fig. 1.13 Legs extended, gently flex toes back toward the head, activating the Bubbling Springs (Kidney 1) point.

The Kidney 1 point, Bubbling Springs

4. **Rest—heat in psoas, energy pooling in soles:** Rest now. Smile to your psoas muscles. Be aware of how the psoas feels. The rest period is very important. Collect the energy. Feel the warmth and heat vibrating in the psoas muscles. Bring your attention to the soles of your feet and feel a pool of energy gathering there and rising up.

5. **Repeat:** Beginning again with an inhale and flexing the toes, repeat this movement a few times.

○ Activating the Lao Gong Pericardium Points

1. **Inhale—flex soles, rotate ankles, make fists:** Inhale, flex your feet and curl your toes toward your head, and rotate your ankles so that the soles are facing one another. Close your hands into fists and press into your palms with your middle fingers at the Lao Gong points, the pericardium points (fig. 1.14).

2. **Exhale—sink chest to spine, lumbars to mat:** Exhale, relaxing feet and fists and chest. Feel the heart sink down toward the spine as you lightly press your lumbar spine to the mat. Feel the heat from the hands flow up the arms and shoulders to the spine and down to thoracic vertebrae T5

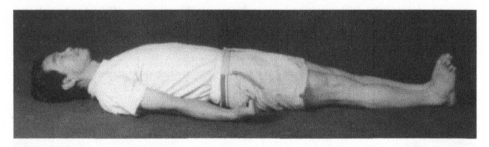

Fig. 1.14 Flex your feet and rotate your ankles. Make fists and press your middle fingers into the Lao Gong points.

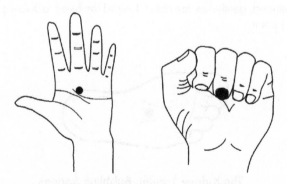

The Pericardium 8 point, Lao Gong

and T6 between the scapulae. At the same time, feel the heat from the heart/pericardium flow down your spine to T5–T6. Now feel this heat at T5–T6 flow down the spine to the psoas muscles and kidneys and finally to the soles of your feet. Feel your psoas muscles receiving the heat, getting nice and warm, releasing any contractions, and energizing the lower back. Do this a few more times.

3. **Rest:** Smile to your organs as you enjoy the sensations throughout your whole body. This would be a good time to enjoy a few minutes of the Lotus Meditation, the next exercise in this first set.

Lotus Meditation

The Lotus Meditation can be used during Tao Yin practice and is especially useful during the rest periods between exercises. You can use either the Lotus Meditation or Full-Body Breathing during any rest period. The Lotus Meditation helps to balance the kidney and heart energies, which is a vital part of self-healing. The balanced flow of water and fire energy greatly helps in transforming accumulated stress in the mind and body into a sense of well-being.

In a pond several lotus plants join together in a cluster, anchoring in the mud. In this meditation, imagine the heart as a red lotus flower and the pericardium (the heat-regulating membrane that encloses the heart) as the lotus pads. Visualize the kidneys as the bulbs where the stems of the pads and the lotus flower join. Visualize roots extending from the kidneys down through the legs into the watery mud of the earth.

Through this dreamscape imagery sense various qualities of energy in your body. Feel the supporting connection of the warm red energy of the heart and the golden energy coming to you from the sun and the universe above. Likewise, sense the cool, blue water energy of the kidneys and the refreshing blue water energy from the earth.

1. **Sitting tall, breathe to the tan tien:** Breathe to the tan tien and consider the lovely blooming lotus. See the open flower as red with yellow/gold petals in the center.
2. **Look at the pads, stem, and roots:** The lotus leaves float on the water's surface. See the stem as it descends to the roots in the mud. Feel the roots sinking into the bed of the pond, all the way down to the kidneys. The roots receive just the correct amount of nutrition from the wet earth.

Lotus/Heart/Kidney Energy Dreamscape. Balancing the kidney and heart energies is vital to self-healing. Imagine the heart as a red lotus flower and the pericardium (the heat-regulating membrane that encloses the heart) as the lotus pads. Visualize the kidneys as bulbs, similar to the clusters where the stems of the pads and the lotus flower join. Several lotus plants usually join together in a cluster, anchoring the mud. From the kidneys (kidney bulbs/clusters), visualize roots extending down through the legs into the watery mud of the earth basin. Feel the warm red energy of the heart and the red and yellow/gold from above. Likewise, sense the cool, blue water energy of the kidneys and the refreshing blue water energy from the earth.

3. **Sense the harmony of fire and water:** The pads and flower open to the sun to soak up the life-sustaining rays. The sun is the source of fire energy. The earth holds the necessary water. Appreciate this life-giving harmony of the forces of fire and water, yang and yin, male and female.

4. **Connect images with your heart and kidneys:** As you continue with the tan tien breath, expanding and contracting, look inside to your heart and kidneys. The kidneys are the roots accessing water. The heart is the open lotus taking in the sun's fiery gift. The spine is the healthy and supple stem connecting the two energies.

5. **Inhale to the heart and exhale to the kidneys:** Coordinate the tan tien breathing: Inhale into the heart, drawing warmth from the sun; feel that warmth come down through the crown of the head and blend it with the love, joy, and happiness in the red heart/lotus. As you slowly inhale, draw this loving, hot heart energy back to the point opposite the heart center on the spine (the Wing point, between the scapulae, or between T5 and T6) as you slowly inhale. Then exhale the hot energy down the lotus stem/spine to the cool kidneys, warming them with the loving heat from the heart. You may enhance the emotional balancing effect by subvocally exhaling with the heart sound, "Haw-w-w-w-w" (from the Cosmic Healing Sounds meditation) as you mentally direct the heart energy down the spine.

6. **Inhale into the kidneys and exhale up to the heart:** See the kidneys as the nourishing bulbs of the lotus with roots that extend down through the legs and soles of the feet into the mud, accessing the soothing blue water energy held by the earth. As you inhale to the kidneys, feel that the roots are drawing the cool, soothing, nourishing blue water energy up through the soles of the feet, up through the legs to the kidneys. In the kidneys, feel the gentle, peaceful feeling blending with the cool, soothing blue water energy that has percolated up through the legs. As you exhale, you can subvocally express the kidney sound, "Cho-o-o-o-o," and send this soothing boost of gentle, cooling, wet, blue kidney energy up through the supple stem/spine via the wing point to the grateful, happy heart.

7. **Continue alternating the breath this way a few times:** Red light from the crown into the heart and down to the kidneys; blue light from Bubbling Springs into the kidneys and up to the heart.

8. **Relax:** Now simply move the smiling mind back and forth between the heart and kidneys along the connecting spinal stem; don't bother about the breath. The balancing will automatically occur. Smile to the lotus in its perfection and beauty. Smile with gratitude to your kidneys, spine, and heart.

The Lotus Meditation is very calming. Naturally, the more it is practiced, the easier it is to realize this inner calm.

 ### Monkey Rests with Knees in Air
Meridians activated: Meridians of the leg—
Spleen, Kidney, and Liver (all yin)

1. **Place knees to chest, palms on inside of legs:** Bring your knees toward your chest and let your feet hang. Place your palms on the inside of the legs, just below the knees. Spread your legs evenly apart, then let gravity pull the knees apart so you begin to feel the stretch of the psoas muscle evenly on both sides (fig. 1.15).

2. **Inhale, then exhale from heart to psoas:** The most important part of this exercise is the breathing. Take an inhale. Then exhale the heat from the heart down to your psoas muscle and to that part of the iliopsoas complex that connects to the thigh on the inside of your groin. As you feel the muscles, breathe into them gently to release any tension that may be stored there. Breathe through the tension and relax. Try to lengthen the muscle so that the two sides are even.

3. **Hold inside shins or ankles:** As you become comfortable in this position, extend your arms to hold inside your shins and eventually inside your ankles (fig. 1.16). Breathe into the muscles, exhaling any gray, cloudy energy and inhaling golden light. Smile and enjoy the sensations.

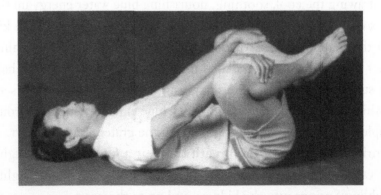

Fig. 1.15 With hands below knees, let the knees part to stretch the psoas muscle evenly on both sides.

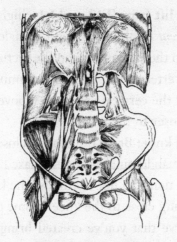

The iliopsoas muscle

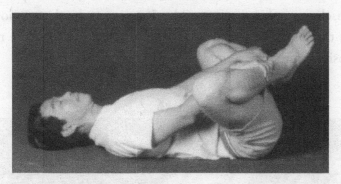

Fig. 1.16 Hold shins or ankles. Exhale heat from the heart down to the psoas muscle at its connection on the inside of the groin.

 Crocodile Lifts Head
Meridian activated: Bladder (yang)

The most important note about this exercise is not to lift up the head first, but instead to raise up from the lower thoracic vertebrae. The crocodile cannot lift the head without the lower body.

1. **Bring knee to chest:** Inhale, bringing your left knee up toward your chest and clasping both hands over your knee (fig. 1.17). Extend your right leg along the floor (or you may choose to bend at the knee slightly to be more comfortable during the lift). Don't apply any force to your bent knee, such as pulling on it. Just hold the knee in a relaxed way.

Set 1:
Foundations

67

2. **Scoop sacrum and lift from T12 and L1:** Slightly tuck the chin to lock the neck (see *Comment* on the next page). Exhale as you press your lumbar spine down onto the mat and scoop the sacrum, then lift up from the low back (thoracic vertebra T12 and upper lumbar L1) (fig. 1.18). Feel a slight curving along the cervical vertebrae (above T12). Allow that curve to bring the head closer to the knee.

3. **Bring head toward knee:** Bring the head as close to your knee as is comfortable. Keep your abdominal muscles relaxed and maintain a smiling sensation in the tan tien. Do not try to kiss the knee; there are no bonus points for even getting close to the knee! Come only as close to the knee as the vertebral curve that you've created brings you. Don't stick your head out or lead with your head. Maintain awareness of the smiling sensation in your second brain in your lower tan tien, and keep the abdominal muscles as relaxed as possible. Keep your lumbar region pressed toward the floor and feel your sacrum raised slightly off the mat. Hold that position for a few seconds.

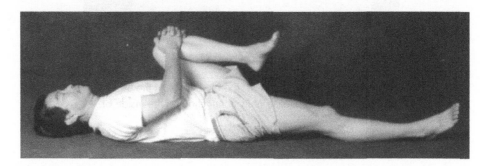

Fig. 1.17 Bring the left knee up toward the chest, right leg extended.

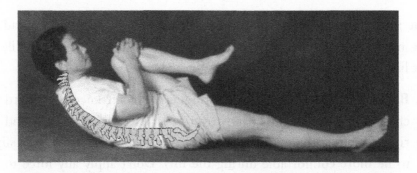

Fig. 1.18 Exhale and press the lumbar spine to the mat, then lift the spine from T12 and L1.

4. **Release:** Inhale and come down to the floor gently, feeling the thoracic vertebrae touch down one by one, maintaining soft flexibility.

5. **Rest:** Rest and smile down to the psoas muscles, which were activated in the lift.

6. **Repeat:** Do a few repetitions of this movement on one side, then repeat with the same number of repetitions on the other side of the body.

   Comment: To help the head not to lead, try the following. Tuck the chin back slightly so that you can feel the neck muscles tighten a bit. Now the cervical vertebrae are "locked" in place, which means that the head cannot initiate a movement; it can only follow. Be careful not to create tension in the neck. Tuck the chin back, but not too much. After coming to the fully raised position, it is okay to move the head a little more in order to release tension from the back of the neck and to feel the neck a bit more relaxed.

 ## Monkey Clasps Knees
Meridian activated: Bladder (yang)

1. **Bend knees, raise sacrum and thoracics:** Bend your knees, clasping your hands over your knees. Tuck your chin gently toward your chest, then exhale as you press the lumbar spine down onto the mat and allow the sacrum and thoracic vertebrae to lift off the floor (fig. 1.19). Tuck the chin slightly to avoid leading with the head as your body lifts up off the mat with the lumbars pressed down.

2. **Press knees up, maintaining psoas awareness:** As you continue to press the lumbar area of the spine into the mat, press your knees against the counterforce of your hands and arms to activate the psoas.

3. **Raise your sacrum and your thoracic vertebrae:** With the psoas and iliopsoas muscles activated, remember to maintain awareness of the smiling sensation in your lower tan tien and check that your abdominal muscles are

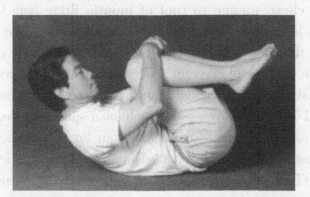

Fig. 1.19 Clasping your bent knees, press the lumbar spine to the floor, allowing the sacrum and the thoracic spine to lift off the floor.

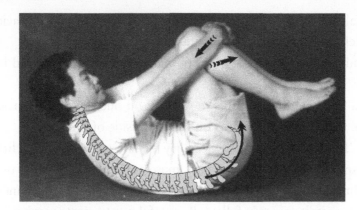

Fig. 1.20 Pressing knees against hands to activate psoas and iliopsoas, raise your sacrum and thoracic vertebrae.

relatively relaxed. Feel your lumbar spine pressing into the mat as you raise your sacrum and your thoracic vertebrae (fig. 1.20). Do not raise your head and upper body any further—if you raise your head and upper body, you are not doing the exercise properly. Notice your iliopsoas and psoas muscles as you do this exercise. (Don't get discouraged if this doesn't come easily. Awareness grows with practice.) Hold without straining for several seconds.

4. **Release and rest:** Release on an inhale and rest. Relax as you breathe in golden energizing light.
5. **Repeat:** Repeat this exercise several times.

 ## Monkey Pushes against Knees
Meridians activated: Heart (yin) and Small Intestine (yang)

In the following exercise you will be clenching your teeth and pressing the tip of your tongue against the roof of your mouth. There is an important connection between the teeth, the tongue, the heart, and the psoas muscle. By clenching your teeth and pressing your tongue against the roof of your mouth, you are increasing the power that can be generated by the psoas muscle. This will also help activate the cranial pump; it is an internal power process.

1. **Bring knees to chest, tongue to roof of mouth:** Bring both knees toward the chest, letting your feet dangle above the buttocks. Rest both hands just above the knees. Slightly tuck your chin toward your chest. Clench your teeth a little and press the tip of the tongue to the roof of your mouth to make the internal connection to the heart and the psoas.
2. **Raise up from T6:** Exhale as you press the lumbar spine into the mat and raise the sacrum off the mat slightly; use your lower back muscles (specifically the psoas) to initiate this movement. Raise the thoracic vertebrae from T6. (The sixth thoracic vertebra, between the scapulae and

opposite the heart center at the front of the spine, is referred to as the Wing point, and is also known as the Wind point for the Heart meridian.) This movement will allow the shoulders to be raised slightly off the floor. Keep the chin tucked and the lower thoracic vertebrae, from T7 to T12, pressed to the mat along with the lumbar spine.

3. **Connect tongue, heart, T6, and hands:** Press your knees against your hands and press the hands against the knees, balancing the counterforces (fig. 1.21). Keep your elbows locked so that the force directed through the arms comes from the Wind point at T6 through the scapulae and shoulders. Also feel the connection of force from the tongue to the heart and T6.

4. **Inhale and relax:** Smile and feel chi moving through your lower back and the psoas muscle.

5. **Repeat:** Repeat this exercise several times. Finally, lower the legs to the mat and practice conscious breathing as you rest.

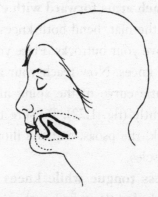

Press tongue on roof behind teeth

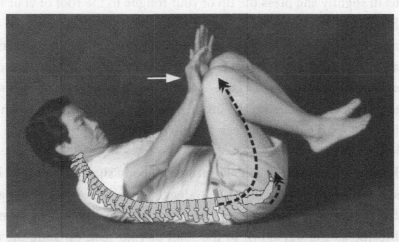

Fig. 1.21 Raise the thoracic vertebrae from T6, the point behind the heart. Press knees against hands and hands against knees, balancing counterforces. Connect tongue, heart, T6, and heels of hands.

Comment: Do not press from the knees with the muscle power of the legs. Instead, transfer the power from the lower lumbars and the psoas muscles through your skeletal structure. This is very important. By generating the force for the movement from your lumbar region and transferring the force through the activated psoas muscles to the thighbones and thus to the knees, resisting with your hands strengthens the psoas muscles. The lumbar vertebrae open into a straight line as the lower spine straightens, allowing the lumbar force to be effectively directed through the thighbones to the knees.

If you do these exercises properly you will be able to practice tai chi and all of the other exercises more effectively, generating the movement from the psoas and lumbar region.

Monkey Prays with Elbows

1. **Reach arms forward with elbows between knees:** Keeping your back on the mat, bend both knees toward your chest, letting the feet dangle above your buttocks. Place your elbows so that they touch the insides of the knees. Now reach your arms forward, palms together, and feel the gentle curve of the spine lift your thoracic spine and neck and head slightly (fig. 1.22). Be sure to initiate the thoracic lift from the lower back, the psoas, and the iliopsoas muscles—not from the knees or leg muscles.

2. **Press tongue while knees and elbows counter push:** Clench your teeth slightly and press the tip of your tongue to the roof of your mouth. Exhale as you press the lumbar spine down, raise the sacrum, and lift the body from T12. Now press your legs together as you resist with your arms (fig. 1.23). Keep your belly muscles relatively soft and relaxed. Your elbows push out and your knees push in. Make sure that you're not using the adductor muscles on the inside of your thighs. Instead, use the lumbar region to push your legs together. Don't forget your smile in the lower tan tien!

3. **Repeat, then rest:** Inhale, lowering the body slowly, and relax. Repeat several times, then lower the legs and do conscious breathing. Experience the sensation in the back, especially the psoas muscle. Breathe all the way down to the soles of your feet, exhaling the cloudy gray color. Inhale the golden light to the areas you feel most affected. When you breathe you are conducting the chi, bringing nutrients and energy to the psoas muscles.

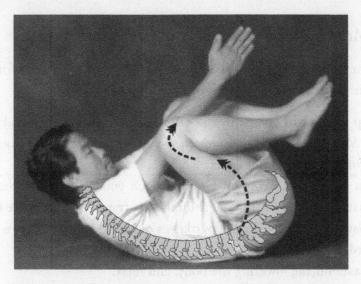

Fig. 1.22 With elbows pressing on knees, reach the arms forward and lift through the thoracic spine, initiating the movement from the psoas and iliopsoas.

Fig. 1.23 Press tongue to roof of mouth. Pressing the lumbar spine down, raise the sacrum and thoracics and then press in with the knees while resisting with arms.

Comment: Your mind and tan tien awareness will become more attuned with practice. You will be able to easily direct the force through your structure from the lumbar vertebrae and psoas to the knees. At the start you may experience very little resistance when you do this because the muscles need strengthening to move in this way.

Monkey Prays Counterpose: Clasp Knees

Except for the position of the arms and the direction of the counterforces, this exercise is similar to Monkey Prays with Elbows.

1. **Clasp knees with arms:** Bend both knees toward the chest and separate as in Monkey Prays. Your hands clasp your knees so that the elbows bend comfortably around the knees.
2. **Press knees out, arms in:** Gently clench your teeth, press the tongue against the roof of the mouth, and raise up, transfering the force from the lumbars to the knees. Press your knees outward while your arms exert an inward counterforce.
3. **Release:** Inhale, lowering the body, and relax.
4. **Repeat and rest:** Repeat the movement and then rest.

 ## Twist Body Like a Snake
Meridian activated: Gall Bladder (yang)

1. **Lower knees right:** Lying on your back, bring both knees up and place your feet flat on the mat. Let your knees fall slowly to the right, coming as close to the mat as possible without strain. Extend your left arm to the left side, palm up; put the right hand on the left side of the lower tan tien. Turn your head to the left, leaving both shoulders on the floor (fig. 1.24).
2. **Hold and breathe left:** Rest, smile, and breathe in this position. Breathe with your attention on your left side, inhaling golden energizing light and exhaling a cloudy gray color. Focus on expanding and elongating this area. Remain in this position for a few minutes, breathing with full awareness into your left rib cage, abdomen, lumbar region, hip joint, shoulders, and neck. Smile and send positive energy into the spine.
3. **Return to center:** Slowly bring your knees and head back to center and notice the sensations in your body.
4. **Lower knees left:** Move both knees slowly to the left until they come close to or touch the mat. Turn your head to the right. Extend the right arm out and place the left hand on the right side of the lower tan tien (fig. 1.25).
5. **Hold and breathe right:** Breathe fully into the right side for a few minutes, allowing the right side to elongate and expand. Inhale golden energizing light and exhale a cloudy gray color. Remain in this position for a few minutes, breathing with full awareness into your right rib cage,

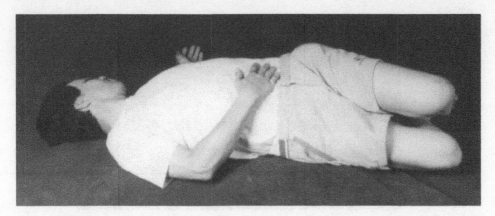

Fig. 1.24 The upper body turns to the left while the lower body turns right. Extend left arm to left side, palm up. Put right hand on left side of tan tien.

Fig. 1.25 The upper body turns to the right while the lower body turns left.

abdomen, lumbar region, hip joint, shoulders, and neck. Smile and send positive energy into the spine.

6. **Return to center:** Bring your knees and head back to the center position and relax. Be aware of all the sensations in your body as you rest on the mat.

7. **Rest:** Lower your legs to the mat and rest comfortably on your back. Relax and smile into your body.

 Monkey Flaps Legs

Meridians activated: Meridians of the leg—
Spleen, Kidney, and Liver (all yin)

1. **Bend knees, soles touching:** Loosening the psoas: Lying on your back, bend your knees and place the soles of your feet together. Hold the feet

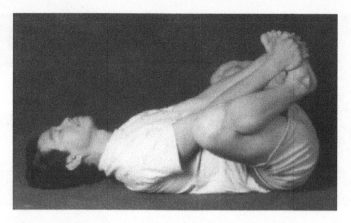

Fig. 1.26 Place the soles of the feet together. Spread the knees apart and gently move the legs back and forth.

Fig. 1.27 Soles together, arms out, move the legs up and down.

together with your hands (fig. 1.26). (If you are unable to reach your feet, you can grasp higher up on the leg.) Spread your knees apart and gently move the legs back and forth, loosening the psoas. Feel the stretch in the groin. Do not bounce too vigorously.

2. **Move knees up and down:** Place the arms out to the sides, palms down. Place your legs on the floor with the soles touching (fig. 1.27). Keep the lumbar spine flat on the mat. Move the knees up and down.

3. **Relax:** Smile and breathe into your groin. Relax your legs. Stay in this position for as long as you wish, loosening the psoas muscle.

4. **Release and rest:** Bring your knees up and then extend your legs long on the mat. Feel the enlivened energy in your hips, groin, and legs.

Comment: It may take a while before you are able to comfortably lower your knees closer to the mat with the soles of the feet together without needing to hold your feet with your hands. Be patient and practice.

8

Set 2
More Spine and Psoas Conditioning, Lymph Laughing, and Ring-Muscle Power

As with set 1, all of the following exercises begin lying on the back. These exercises provide more conditioning and training for the spine and psoas muscle. The spine is flexed and extended up off the mat, balancing the downward movement of flexions in set 1. One exercise promotes the opening of the Wing point for relieving blockages behind the heart. The internal connection of the tongue to major tendons throughout the body is strengthened, developing greater internal power. Finally, the connection between the psoas muscle and the major sphincters in the body, the "ring muscles," is activated, establishing greater internal power and harmony. Coordinating the body's ring-muscle network with the psoas muscle moves chi throughout the body and is valuable training for developing one's Yi, the mind-eye-heart power.

Exercises in This Set
1. Stretch the Bow 1 and 2
2. Mountain Rises from Sea
3. Cricket Rests on Flower
4. Snake Turns at Wing Point
5. Baby Playing and Laughing
6. Swallow Opens Its Feathers
7. Monkey Hugs Knees 1 and 2

Stretch the Bow 1 and 2

This exercise develops the psoas and abdominal muscles in a balanced way. Be mindful that if you lift the upper body too much, you are doing Full Bow, the movement instructed in part 2.

Part 1: Balanced Bow
Meridian activated: Bladder (yang)

1. **Press lumbars to mat and raise legs:** Lie flat on your back, legs straight out in front of you, arms at your sides palms down. Take three to four long, deep breaths. Press your lumbar spine to the mat and raise your legs slightly off the floor, initiating the movement from the hips. Raise the upper body at the same time.
2. **Stretch arms to feet, raise thoracics and neck and head:** Keeping your lumbar spine firmly on the floor, exhale and stretch your arms toward your feet while you lift the legs about six inches off the floor. Tuck your chin and raise your thoracics, then your neck and head (fig. 2.1). Don't worry about how high you can lift your legs and don't try to touch your toes.
3. **Hold, then release:** Hold the raised position briefly at the end of the exhale, and then inhale, letting the entire body relax slowly down to the mat. Rest briefly.
4. **Repeat:** Repeat this movement two times.
5. **Rest:** When you finish, rest for a few minutes, feeling the warmth and energy in your lumbar area. Smile to the whole spine and enjoy the sensations streaming through your body.

Part 2: Full Bow
Meridian activated: Heart (yin)

1. **Press lumbars to mat and raise legs:** Lie flat on your back, legs straight out in front of you, arms at your sides palms down. Take three to four long, deep breaths. Press your lumbar spine to the mat and then raise your legs slightly off the floor, initiating the movement from the hips. Raise the upper body at the same time.
2. **Lift torso and legs, stretch tongue:** This time as you exhale raise your entire torso off the floor at the same time as you raise your legs high. Balance legs and upper body on your buttocks. At the same time stretch your tongue out as much as you can (fig. 2.2). Really feel the stretch!

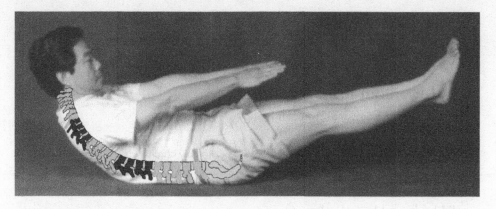

Fig. 2.1 With the lumbar spine and sacrum flat on the mat, simultaneously raise the legs, thoracics, and head.

Fig. 2.2 Raise the legs and upper body simultaneously and stretch out the tongue.

3. **Stretch from scapulae through fingers and through heels, flex toes:** Stretch forward from your scapulae to your fingertips; stretch through your heels and flex your toes toward your head so that you feel the stretch through your legs and feet. Curving this way through the middle of your body, feel the stretch in the psoas muscle complex from the lumbar spine and the sacrum to the connections at the femur bones. With practice you will be able to touch your toes. Feel the connection between the tongue and all the major tendons throughout the body affected by this full stretch from head to foot.
4. **Relax:** Inhale and relax back to the mat. Enjoy the refreshing sensations streaming throughout your body.

Set 2:
Spine and Psoas
Conditioning

5. Repeat and rest: Repeat two or three times, then rest and do some conscious breathing or practice Lotus Meditation for a few minutes.

 ## Mountain Rises from Sea
Meridian activated: Stomach (yang)

Caution: If you have high blood pressure, please be extremely careful while doing this exercise.

The mountain is very solid and stable. Be a mountain on the sea's horizon—a solid body, stable and calm.

1. **Tilt sacrum upward, follow with L5:** Lie on your back, arms at your sides, palms down, knees bent, and feet flat on the floor. Exhale as you tilt your sacrum upward. Let the lowest lumbar vertebra, L5, follow the sacrum, rising upward.
2. **Follow with lumbar vertebrae:** One by one, very slowly bring each lumbar vertebra up off the mat.
3. **Follow with thoracic vertebrae:** One by one, raise each thoracic vertebrae from the mat until you come to the cervical vertebrae. Keep your neck and head flat on the mat as you begin to roll up onto your shoulders (fig. 2.3).
4. **Lift high:** Let your body reach as high as you can comfortably go. Continue breathing deeply. Hold this position for a few moments.
5. **Come down vertebra by vertebra:** Now slowly bring the spine down vertebra by vertebra. First bring the thoracic vertebrae gently to the mat, then the lumbar vertebrae, and finally the sacrum. As you descend, notice which vertebrae touch the mat individually and which touch the mat as a

Fig. 2.3 Beginning with the sacrum, lift the spine as high as possible, keeping the head and neck flat on the mat.

group. Feel the space between each vertebra open and feel the chi flow in. This movement requires mindfulness, so go slowly. (After gaining some awareness and proficiency in this process, you can adjust your rate of movement and your breathing pattern.)

6. **Repeat:** Repeat the movement once.

7. **Rest:** Now rest, smile to the whole spine, and relax. Let a sense of well-being spread throughout the whole body. Smile and breathe golden energy through the spine and into every cell in your body.

 ## Cricket Rests on Flower

Meridians activated: Stomach (yang) and Pericardium (yin)

Caution: Discontinue this exercise if it causes you serious discomfort!

Sense the delicacy, control, and balance implied by the name Cricket Rests on Flower, yet retain the sense of calm, solid structure from the previous exercise as you proceed into this movement.

1. **Raise vertebrae through cervicals, place hands, roll to crown:** Begin by lying on your back, arms at your sides, palms down. Keep your feet flat on the mat as you bend your knees. Exhale as you raise the sacrum, lumbar, and thoracic vertebrae off the floor very slowly, as in the previous exercise, Mountain Rises from Sea. Continue the movement with normal breathing. When you come to the cervical vertebrae, place your palms flat on the floor overhead, fingers pointing toward your feet. Roll from the base of your skull to the crown of your head (fig. 2.4). Make sure your entire backside is lifted off the mat—only your feet, hands, and crown make contact with the mat.

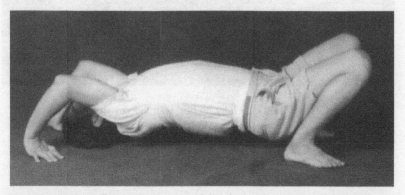

Fig. 2.4 Raise each vertebra starting from the sacrum, then roll from the back of the head to the crown. Only the feet, hands, and crown make contact with the mat.

2. **Inhale and roll down:** Inhale and slowly roll back down, first through the head and neck and then through the thoracic vertebrae, then through the lumbar spine, and finally through the sacrum. Come down one vertebra at a time, breathing naturally.

3. **Exhale and raise:** Exhale as you slowly raise the sacrum, lumbar spine, the hips, and the thoracic area slowly, one vertebra at a time. When you come to the top of your thoracic spine, hold for a moment.

4. **Inhale and roll down:** Inhale and come down slowly. Rest. Breathe and smile to your entire spine. Inhale golden energy into the spine and exhale any cloudy, gray-colored, negative energy.

5. **Exhale and raise through crown:** Exhale slowly and come all the way up now, raising one vertebra at a time: first the sacrum, then the hips, the lumbar spine, the thoracic spine, the cervical spine, and roll through the skull to the crown of the head (fig. 2.5). Be a beautiful cricket! Rise up fully and hold, staying in your comfort zone for up to one minute.

6. **Inhale and roll down:** Inhale slowly and then begin coming back down, each vertebra touching the mat one by one.

7. **Rest:** Rest. Smile, noticing how your body feels. Breathe consciously as you enjoy the sensations streaming through your body.

Fig. 2.5 Full Cricket: The body fully arched with the crown on the mat

Snake Turns at Wing Point
Meridian activated: Triple Warmer (yang)

The Gia Pe, or Wing point, is between the shoulder blades in the midthoracic area. Located behind the sternum on the spine, between thoracic vertebrae 5 and 6, Wing point lies opposite (or on the back side of) the heart center. The area around the Gia Pe is called the back *pakua*, while the region around the sternum or breastbone is called the front pakua. Women may experience stagnant energy in these areas because of pressure from wearing a bra and the consequent compression of the breast tissue. Blockage in these areas can lead to many forms of pain and sickness.

Snake Turns at Wing Point opens the meridians connecting the front and back pakuas via the heart center, clearing the channels for the free flow of energy down the back to the kidneys and then down to the ovaries and the prostate gland. Opening these meridians will prevent sickness stuck in the back from spreading to the front. This exercise is also effective in helping men to open the heart.

When practicing this exercise move only the upper back. Feel the back pakua open. Feel the warmth and chi throughout your upper back. Feel the Wing point open.

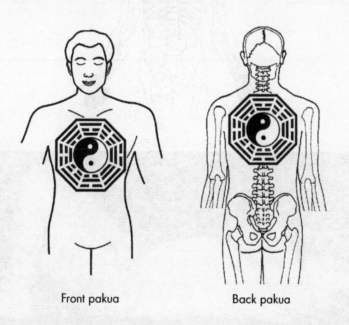

Front pakua   Back pakua

Pakua symbols placed on the heart center and the Wing point

1. **Bend knees, embrace shoulders:** Begin by lying on your back. Embrace yourself, gently grasping the outside of each shoulder. Bend your knees, keeping your feet flat on the mat (fig. 2.6).

2. **Exhale and lift from Gia Pe:** Tuck your chin and exhale while you lift the upper body from the Gia Pe, the Wing point (fig. 2.7).

3. **Twist upper body and head left:** Continuing to exhale and keeping your chin tucked, twist your upper body and head to the left, leaving your lower back on the mat (fig. 2.8). As you turn the upper body be sure that only thoracic vertebrae T1 through T6 are lifted off the mat. Our goal is to open the heart center and the Gia Pe.

4. **Twist right:** Inhale to come back to the center, upper body still lifted. Exhale as you twist your upper body to the right.

5. **Center and release:** Inhale to return to the center position, then release down to the mat. Relax, smile, and bring golden light into the back pakua.

6. **Repeat:** Repeat this exercise three times on each side.

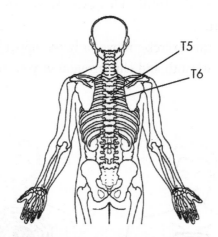

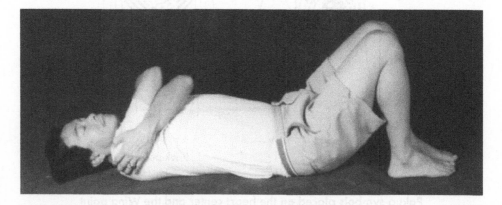

Fig. 2.6 Cross hands over chest, holding each shoulder, knees up.

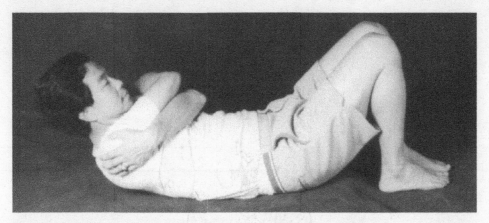

Fig. 2.7 With chin tucked, lift the thoracics from Gia Pė as you exhale.

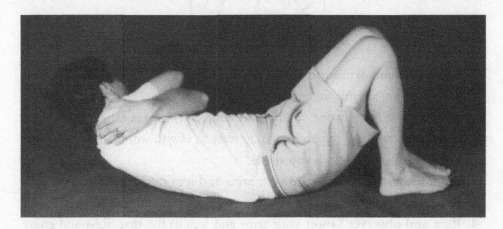

Fig. 2.8 Roll to the left from T5–T6 while still exhaling.

 ## Baby Playing and Laughing

Happy babies often express joy by rolling onto their back and lifting arms and legs in the air. Uninhibited in their movements, they shake their limbs loose and free, cooing, gurgling, and laughing. Baby Playing and Laughing earns its name from this quintessential baby behavior. Laughter increases the secretion of endorphins, which in turn increase oxygenation of the blood. Endorphins also relax the arteries and decrease blood pressure. All of this has a positive effect on cardiovascular and respiratory ailments. Overall, laughter increases the immune system response.

This movement activates the lymph system, draining the lymph (waste from the body's muscular output) from the periphery of the body to the lymph chamber near the heart.

Set 2:
Spine and Psoas
Conditioning

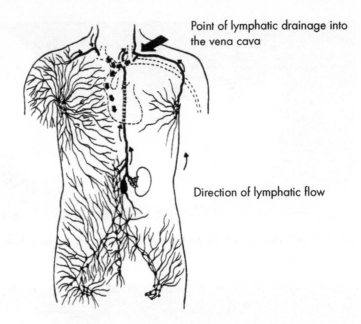

Point of lymphatic drainage into the vena cava

Direction of lymphatic flow

1. **Raise legs and arms and shake:** Lying on your back, raise your legs and arms into the air and shake them like a rag doll (fig. 2.9). Breathe deeply, making tension-releasing sounds and long sighs as you exhale. Shake the body loose and feel the abdomen activate as if you were laughing—even better, begin laughing as you shake.

2. **Stop:** Stop shaking and keep your arms and legs in the air.

3. **Repeat:** Repeat the shaking and rest at least twice more.

4. **Rest and observe:** Lower your arms and legs to the mat. Rest and enjoy the sensation of chi spreading out to the whole body, especially the navel and the lumbar areas. Observe the lymphatic flow from your arms and legs.

Fig. 2.9 Shake the body loose.

Swallow Opens Its Feathers

1. **Lift legs and raise sacrum:** Lying on your back with your legs straight and your arms palms down at your sides, press your lumbar spine into the mat. Using your arms for support, slowly lift your legs straight into the air, raising your sacrum slightly off the mat to balance the effort of the legs and psoas (fig. 2.10).

2. **Lower legs toward floor, press lumbar spine to mat:** Lift your legs as far up as comfortable and then slowly bring them downward. When the heels are about six inches from the mat, hold for a moment and then raise the legs back up again. Make sure to keep your lumbar region pressed against the mat.

3. **Spread legs and draw circles:** Spread your legs apart to a comfortable distance. Now use the psoas and iliopsoas muscles to move your legs slowly in big circles. You can touch your psoas muscle on the inner thigh, close to your groin (fig. 2.11). Keeping your legs straight, make five large, round, smooth circles, left leg clockwise and right leg counterclockwise.

4. **Circle in opposite direction:** Now make five circles in the opposite direction. Let your legs move slowly, keeping your lumbar spine on the mat.

5. **Criss-cross legs:** Now move your legs laterally, criss-crossing back and forth, alternating the front and back legs in the movement (fig. 2.12). Slowly criss-cross the legs several times.

Fig. 2.10 Using your arms as support, lift your legs and press the lumbars down.

6. **Lower legs to floor:** Pressing the lumbar spine to the mat, slowly lower the legs to the floor.

7. **Rest:** Rest and enjoy the sensations streaming through your body. Smile and breathe deeply.

Fig. 2.11 Circle legs five times in the air, left leg clockwise and right leg counterclockwise. Then reverse direction for five more circles.

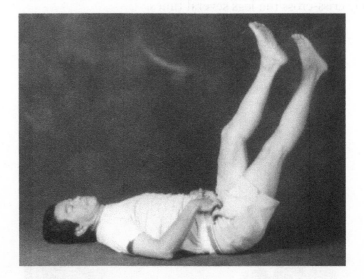

Fig. 2.12 Cross the legs back and forth.

DEVELOPING SPHINCTER-MUSCLE AWARENESS
AND COORDINATION

With this group of movements we integrate the contracting and relaxing effects of the "spiritual muscle" (the thoracic diaphragm) and the "muscle of the soul" (the psoas muscle) with the body's network of sphincters, the "ring muscles." Taoists call the sphincters the "chi muscles."

The ring-shaped muscles that surround the orifices, or openings, of the body are the sphincter muscles. Internally, the orifices are the places where the round muscles of the sphincters protrude through layers of muscle, the diaphragms, that separate one area or surface from another. The sphincter muscles exist both internally and externally; they contract and release, close and open, tighten and relax.

Our lives are part of a continuum, an unbroken chain of openings and closings, contractions and relaxations. It is this coordinated and harmonious contraction and relaxation that initiates breathing, digestion, circulation, elimination, and all muscular motion. There is nothing in the human body that is not affected by the sphincters. Our eyes open and close to see. Our nostrils open and close to breathe. Our mouth opens and closes to eat and drink. Our muscles contract and relax to move. Our hands open and close to grasp or let go. Our heart contracts and relaxes to circulate the blood. The stomach and

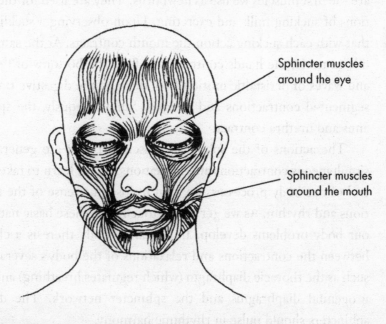

Sphincter muscles around the eye

Sphincter muscles around the mouth

The sphincter muscles of the face and around the eyes and mouth

intestines contract and relax to digest nutrients. When babies open their mouths with their first cries they begin a lifetime of never-ceasing opening and closing of a synchronized system of sphincter muscles. As a life comes to an end, with the final breath the sphincter muscle around the mouth opens, but it does not close. The body ceases to function in the absence of sphincter activity.

The body's sphincter system is the prime mover, the substratum, the source that activates all the body's processes. All the organs, the muscles, the blood circulatory system, the lymphatic system, and the digestive system—everything in the body owes its functionality to the sphincter muscles. All muscles work by contracting and releasing; there is a relationship between the network of circular sphincter muscles and every other system in the body. In a healthy body, all of the sphincter muscles contract and relax simultaneously in a natural pulsing rhythm. Taoists recognized the harmonious action of this primary sphincter system as the mechanism for energizing every cell with vital chi.

The sphincters are a basic structural form in all animal life, including complex human beings, and can be traced back to the simplest prehistoric amoeba. The primitive aspect of the human brain, sometimes referred to as the reptilian brain, functions generally at the subconscious level. The reptilian brain maintains and regulates all the essential survival processes: all muscular movements, breathing, circulation, digestion, and elimination. This brain is intimately connected to the sphincter muscles. The sphincter muscles are the first muscles we use as newborns. They are used for the basic life functions of sucking milk and excreting. Upon observing a suckling baby, notice that with each sucking action the mouth contracts. At the same time the eyelids contract, the hands contract into fists, the bottoms of the feet contract, and waves of peristaltic motion flow through the digestive tract in a series of segmented contractions and releases. Simultaneously, the sphincters of the anus and urethra contract.

The actions of the sphincter muscle network are generally involuntary simultaneous contractions and relaxations. As we learn to take voluntary control of our body processes, we tend to lose our sense of the natural connections and rhythm. As we get out of touch with these basic natural rhythms in our body problems develop. In a healthy body there is a close connection between the contractions and relaxations of the body's several diaphragms—such as the thoracic diaphragm (which regulates breathing) and the pelvic and urogenital diaphragms and the sphincter network. The diaphragms and sphincters should pulse in rhythmic harmony.

During sleep, our eyelids move in rhythm with our breathing. When we exhale, our eyelids contract slightly; when we inhale, they relax and expand slightly. This never-ending chain of contractions and relaxations is subtle, but it is movement. This slight movement goes through the entire body, including the limbs and organs. It is a form of basic, natural exercise. Like recharging a battery, the movement reflected in the eyelids in sleep fills us with vital force, chi.

When sphincter weakness exists in one or more areas of the body, those sphincters can be strengthened by exercising the sphincters that are stronger. When a person loses the natural interconnectedness and rhythm of the sphincter network, retraining can restore proper functioning. For example, by focusing on the eyelid sphincter exercise you can establish a link and help to develop a weak urethral sphincter (which may have resulted in the condition of urinary incontinence).

The two lower sphincters at the front and backside, the sphincters of the urethra and anus, are the major sphincters of the body. The effects of their contractions are felt throughout the body and are key to transporting chi in

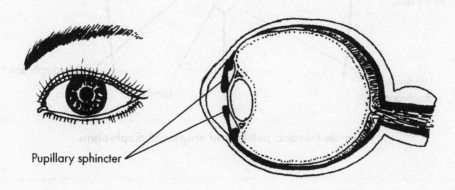

Pupillary sphincter

A cross-section of the human eye. The pupillary sphincter of the iris, near the pupil, contracts in bright light to reduce the pupil area.

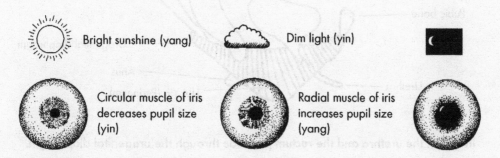

Bright sunshine (yang)   Dim light (yin)

Circular muscle of iris decreases pupil size (yin)   Radial muscle of iris increases pupil size (yang)

The action of the pupillary sphincter. The pupillary sphincter within the iris forms a ring around the pupil at the border of the iris. The contractile membrane of the iris retracts in dim light, opening the pupil area more.

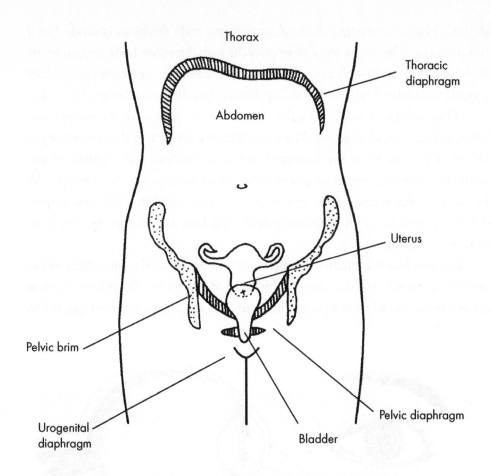

Female thoracic, pelvic, and urogenital diaphragms

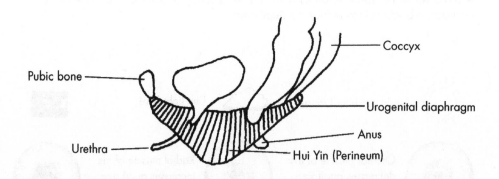

In males, the urethra and the rectum protrude through the urogenital diaphragm.

the lower body upward to the brain. When it is healthy, the anal sphincter is clearly the strongest.

When an infant suckles, the eyes, mouth, anus, and perineum contract. These contractions gradually activate all the involuntary muscles of the body. The heart, the veins, and the arteries are also ring-shaped (round) muscles. The ring muscles in the body—the mouth, eyes, anus, urogenital and pelvic diaphragms, and the perineum—are all interrelated. When these muscles are activated they also activate the psoas muscle. Monkey Hugs Knees is designed to connect the ring muscles with the psoas to establish these interconnections and develop natural internal power and harmony.

The following exercises are divided into two sections. The first section focuses on developing awareness of the individual sphincter muscles and then linking their movements together. This is done by first isolating each area to develop awareness and then linking them into one unified movement. These exercises will help to achieve strength, balance, and coordination of the sphincter muscles. The second section incorporates the coordinated sphincter movements into the psoas movement presented earlier in the chapter. The goal is to link the natural rhythm of the sphincters with the diaphragm and psoas contractions so that they all pulse together in natural harmony. Ultimately, everything is interconnected. You may at some point experience the body unified in automatic movement.

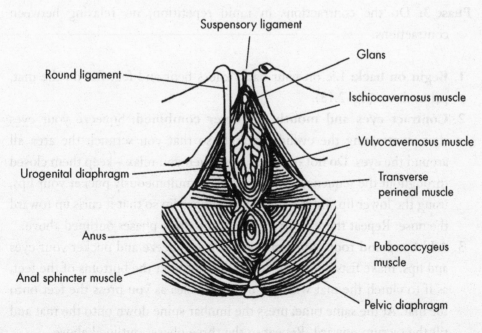

Suspensory ligament

Round ligament

Glans

Ischiocavernosus muscle

Vulvocavernosus muscle

Urogenital diaphragm

Transverse perineal muscle

Anus

Pubococcygeus muscle

Anal sphincter muscle

Pelvic diaphragm

The female chi muscle

Monkey Hugs Knees, Part 1

The following exercise is meant to accommodate practitioners at different stages of awareness, body condition, experience, and ability. Choose what is best for your needs in order to achieve your goals with the most efficient use of your time and energy. You can formulate your own strategy over a longer period of time to systematically develop awareness of all the sphincters and to strengthen, coordinate, and balance them. If you have already achieved significant results with your sphincter system from previous training, you may prefer to move ahead and concentrate on the more advanced stages of practice.

The overall strategy of the exercises is to isolate individual sphincters to develop awareness, even though they are all, in fact, linked. One sphincter may activate the connection to others. Weak connections may be strengthened by stronger ones. Be patient and know that results often come indirectly. Proceed within the limits of your comfort zone.

Each of the following exercises is presented in three phases. Perform each phase three to nine times as outlined below. The contractions are performed during exhalation.

Phase 1: Contract, hold, then relax and inhale (five to ten seconds per round).

Phase 2: Do a series of double contractions, the second stronger and faster than the first.

Phase 3: Do the contractions in rapid repetition, no relaxing between contractions.

1. **Begin on back:** Lie on your back, knees bent and feet flat on the mat, palms down (fig. 2.13).

2. **Contract eyes and mouth sphincter combined:** Squeeze your eyes shut, contracting the eyelids strongly so that you scrunch the area all around the eyes. Do not open the eyes when you relax—keep them closed throughout the sequence. As you exhale, simultaneously pucker your lips, using the lower lip and jaw to push the upper lip so that it curls up toward the nose. Repeat these contractions in the three phases outlined above.

3. **Add hand and foot contractions:** As you squeeze and pucker your eyes and lips, make fists with your hands and contract the bottoms of the feet, as if to clutch the mat with the toes and soles as you press the feet onto the mat. At the same time, press the lumbar spine down onto the mat and tilt the sacrum upward. Repeat in the three phases outlined above.

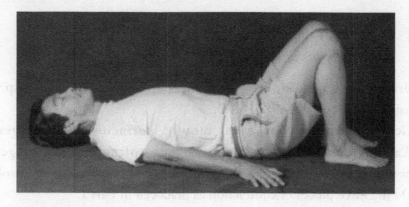

Fig. 2.13 Perform sphincter contractions lying on the back, knees bent and arms at sides.

Comment: The hands and feet muscles are not sphincters, but they affect the sphincters and stimulate sphincter actions.

4. **Contract lower front sphincter (urethral sphincter):** Contract the urethral sphincter in the same way that you stop the flow of urine. Just concentrate on this one sphincter. Try to separate it from the anal sphincter. Repeat the three phases of contractions. As you contract the sphincter, press the lumbar spine down and raise the sacrum. Then rest and smile to the lumbar area to relax the urethral sphincter. Observe your body sensations and the flow of chi throughout the body.

5. **Contract the anal sphincter:** (The anal sphincter consists of two ring muscles, an interior muscle and an exterior muscle). Similar to the front sphincter, squeeze the anus with the interior and exterior components of the anal sphincter, as if resisting the impulse to defecate. This muscle is usually much stronger than the urethral sphincter. Execute the contractions as you simultaneously press the lumbar spine to the mat and lift the sacrum. Complete the three phases of contraction as described earlier. Rest and smile to the areas affected and observe your sensations.

6. **Contract the front and rear sphincters simultaneously:** Now contract the urethral and anal sphincters simultaneously in combination with the lumbar and sacrum movement. Do the three phases of contraction, then rest, smile, and observe.

7. **Contract eyes, mouth, hands and feet, front and rear sphincters simultaneously:** Finally, combine all the contractions with the lumbar and sacrum movement. Practice the three phases of contraction, then rest, smile, and observe.

Set 2:
Spine and Psoas
Conditioning

Monkey Hugs Knees, Part 2
Meridian activated: Bladder (yang)

1. **Bring knees to chest:** Bring your knees up to your chest and clasp your hands over your knees (fig. 2.14).

2. **Gently contract your eyes, mouth, perineum, and urogenital diaphragm:** Contract your eyes, mouth, perineum, and urogenital diaphragm a few times. The psoas muscle becomes automatically involved. Do the three phases of contraction as practiced in Part 1.

3. **Contract eyes and urogenital diaphragm only; move sacrum and lumbars:** Contract and release the ring muscles of only the eyes and the urogenital diaphragm and then begin to move your lumbars and sacrum up and down. The ring muscle near your sexual organ has a close relationship with the psoas. The ring muscle of the eyes are also related to the ring muscle near the sexual organ. It does not matter if you inhale or exhale as you contract, just continue contracting your eyes and your urogenital diaphragm and then relax. Contract and relax, practicing the three phases of contraction as instructed in Part 1. Contract your eyes and your urogenital diaphragm repeatedly while rocking the sacrum up and down against the mat for a total of five to ten minutes to fully engage the psoas muscle.

4. **Contract mouth and sexual organ with sacrum and lumbar movement:** Now contract only your mouth and your urogenital diaphragm. Notice the difference. Both the mouth and the sexual organ work with the psoas, the back, and the diaphragm. Contract and relax for a few minutes, practicing the three phases of contraction as instructed in Part 1. Notice the connection between the ring muscles, back, diaphragm, and psoas.

Fig. 2.14 The position for Part 2 of the sphincter contractions.

5. **Finally, contract your eyes, mouth, anus, perineum, and urogenital diaphragm together:** Feel how linking all of these ring muscles creates a more powerful contraction. Discover the connection between the eyes, mouth, anus, perineum, urogenital diaphragm, psoas, lumbar spine, and diaphragm. Contract and relax for a few more minutes, practicing the three phases of contraction. Some people will have involuntary contractions while they are relaxing. If this happens let the muscles contract and release by themselves until the automatic contractions stop or you decide to stop them.

6. **Rest with legs on mat:** Rest your legs flat on the mat and feel the chi moving through your whole body. Focus your attention on your internal body experience.

   Comment: The ring muscles throughout the body are also known by Taoists as chi muscles. When activated, as in this exercise, the whole body becomes stimulated with chi. When the chi-muscle network is linked in harmony with the psoas muscle, the muscle of the soul, one may become more conscious of the physical and energetic foundations of Yi, the mind-eye-heart power.

9

Set 3
Spirit of the Love Cobra— Developing Yi

This set of exercises begins in the face-down position, and the last two exercises move to sitting positions. The spine is first flexed up in the lower back, then in the upper and lower back, and finally the upper spine is brought into a full arch position. Sideways spinal movement and upward rotation is introduced in the Peacock. More spinal rotations follow in two sitting positions.

The Cobra's Ritual of Love embodies a series of movements and draws on several elements that were cultivated in previous exercises. Just correctly practicing the outer physical mechanics of form, movement, and breath will result in feeling good. To attain the full benefit of this exercise, the internal connections, dynamics, and Yi—the mind-eye-heart power—must be sensitively coordinated. Then all of your earlier training will be fully rewarded.

Exercises in This Set

1. Dolphin Lifts Tail
2. Flying in Dreams
3. Cobra's Ritual of Love (Simple, Basic, Fancy)
4. Peacock Looks at Its Tail
5. Monkey Rotates Spine to Leg Out
6. Monkey Rotates Spine to Leg In

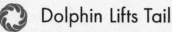 ## Dolphin Lifts Tail

Meridians activated: Bladder (yang) and Kidney (yin)

1. **On belly, tighten buttocks:** Lying on your belly, place your palms down on the mat a few inches in front of your shoulders. Squeeze and tighten your buttocks to protect your lower back.

2. **Lift legs and head:** Exhale as you lift both legs and your head slightly off the mat, arching your back gently.

3. **Return:** Gently return to the floor as you inhale.

4. **Lift and circle legs:** Squeeze the buttocks and exhale as you lift the legs and head again. Make circles with your legs in the air, the legs circling in opposite directions (fig. 3.1).

5. **Return:** Inhale and gently return to the mat. Rest for a breath or two.

6. **Lift and circle legs,** reversing directions: Squeeze your buttocks and lift legs and head again. Repeat the leg circles, reversing the direction of your legs.

7. **Return:** Inhale and return legs and head to the floor.

8. **Lift and "beat" legs:** Exhale, tighten the buttocks and lift head and legs again, and this time "beat" the legs, criss-crossing them from side to side. Alternate sides so that first the right leg crosses on top, then the left leg crosses on top.

9. **Return:** Inhale and return your legs gently to the mat.

10. **Rest and release:** Rest. Breathe consciously into your lumbar vertebrae and completely relax your whole body.

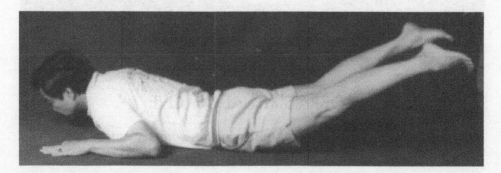

Fig. 3.1 Tighten your buttocks, then lift legs and head. Circle the legs in opposite directions.

Flying in Dreams

Meridians activated: Bladder (yang) and Kidney (yin)

1. **On belly, arms stretched, lift and look up:** Lie on your belly and stretch your arms straight out above your head, palms down. As you exhale lift arms, head, and legs off the floor simultaneously, arching your back. Look up and hold for a few seconds.
2. **Return:** Inhale and lower the body back down to the mat. Relax.
3. **Make fists and lift:** This time as you exhale make fists with your hands, then lift your arms, head, and legs fully off the mat. Arch your back more fully so that only your pubic bone is left touching the floor (fig. 3.2). Hold for a few seconds.
4. **Return:** Inhale and relax.
5. **Repeat:** Repeat this movement sequence a few times.
6. **Release and rest:** After your final repetition, release the body to the floor and relax completely. Smile into and breathe golden light to any part of your body that feels tight or tense. Observe the sensations in your body as you rest on the mat. Release tension, toxins, or tired energy in the form of a cloudy gray color.

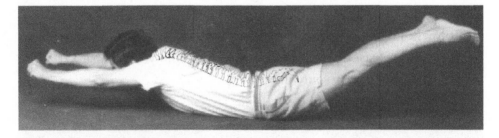

Fig. 3.2 Make fists, then lift and arch the back so that only the pubic bone touches the mat.

COBRA'S RITUAL OF LOVE

This sequence of movements encompasses a few complementary poses. The main movements and poses resemble those of the cobra, famous for its ability to raise itself up from coiled repose and for its interesting mating ritual.

At mating time the king cobra looks for a "queen," tasting the air with his flickering tongue. One king cobra battles another for the nearby queen through ritual neck wrestling. The cobras twine around one another and undulate; the first to push the other's head to the ground wins. The king rubs his chin along the queen's body to calm her and stimulate her for mating; once entwined, they can stay joined for hours. The king helps protect the nest of its brood. When an intruder startles it, the king cobra rears its head, spreads its neck to form a hood, and sways back and forth in a dance of prowess. When he needs to strike to protect, the king cobra will strike quickly.

We have named the raised pose the Love Cobra to distinguish it from the Cobra postures of other disciplines.

The noticeable features of the Tao Yin Love Cobra include the following.

• The raised Love Cobra actively uses the arms to push the body up and to arch the spine. The upper body (above the pubic bone) raises off the mat.
• The Love Cobra tucks the chin, locking the neck vertebrae, to avoid arching the head back.
• The toes stay on the mat to play an important role in the fully raised Love Cobra.
• In the raised position, you roll the eyes up toward the crown of the head and fully extend the tongue with a growl.

The Cobra's Ritual of Love is taught here in three distinct phases. As you begin to learn this exercise, do the Simple Cobra's Love Ritual several times to get the feel of the movement; do the sequence enough so that you can perform it accurately and smoothly, relaxed yet with power. Next, move to the Basic Cobra's Ritual of Love and practice that to assimilate the internal dimensions of the exercise. Read all the descriptive passages for the exercise— you will gain useful insight and information for fleshing out the internal dynamics of the Love Cobra practice. Finally, add in the two extra positions of the Fancy Cobra's Ritual of Love.

 ## Simple Cobra's Ritual of Love
Meridians activated: Stomach (yang) and Heart and Lung (yin)

Use this first level of the exercise to integrate form, movement, and the breath.

1. **Begin on belly:** Lie on your belly with your elbows bent and your palms on the mat. Depending on your body type and condition, your palms can be placed even with your chest or perhaps a little forward of your shoulders. Keep your legs close together, with knees no more than about six inches apart. Press the pads of your toes into the mat.

2. **Push from the toes:** Establish the push from the toes, inhale, and then begin to exhale very slowly. Tighten the buttocks and hold them tight to protect the lower back from strain throughout the lift. (Don't be distracted by the breathing instructions while you are learning the new movements. Stay relaxed and comfortable. Refine your understanding step by step.)

3. **Raise the Love Cobra:** Slowly raise your upper body, keeping your knees, thighs, and pubic bone on the mat. Begin the lift from the lower spine, using the tendons and muscles in the back. Keep them engaged as you complete the lifting in a smooth continuous motion by pushing up more with the arms.

4. **Tuck chin and look up:** Continue to exhale slowly (take a small sip of breath if needed). Tuck your chin lightly as you arch your spine and look up with your eyes. Push the upper body up as far as you can comfortably go but keep the pubic bone on the mat.

5. **Hold—roll eyes, stretch tongue, and gr-r-r-owl:** When your spine is fully arched and you reach the maximum raised stretch, hold everything, roll the eyes up in the sockets, and focus attention at the midcrown. Keeping your eyes rolled upward, stretch your tongue out as far as you can and growl (figs. 3.3 and 3.4). When you have exhaled completely with the growl, hold the breath out just a little longer, stretch the tongue a little more, and intensify your focus at the midcrown point—but don't strain too much.

6. **Release stretch:** Relax the tongue and eyes, keep the buttocks tight, and slowly lower the body back to the mat. When the forehead touches the mat, release the feet so that the tops of the toes rest on the mat. Toe pads and soles relax, facing up.

7. **Back to heels:** Keep the nose close to the mat and push with the forearms, elbows, and palms to move the body back so that the buttocks finally rest on the feet (fig. 3.5). Keep the forearms and hands forward on the mat after they finish pushing. Keep the nose close to the mat's surface. When the buttocks finally settle down on the heels, let the belly and lower chest sink down onto the thighs. Lower the forehead onto the mat and let the whole torso feel as if it is melting into the mat. Enjoy the sensations coursing through your body and breathe consciously to fully relax and refresh.

8. **Forward into Love Cobra lift:** After a brief rest, exhale and lift the forehead and chest up so that the nose is just off the mat. Lift the buttocks off the heels and inhale as you move the torso forward (fig. 3.6). Shift the toes and feet back into the toe-push position. With the nose close to the mat, slide the outstretched hands and forearms forward on the mat to the Love

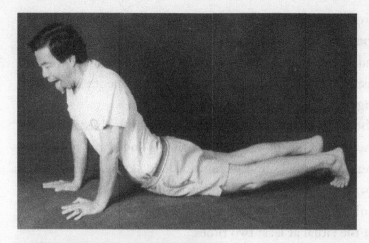

Fig. 3.3
The raised Love
Cobra

Fig. 3.4 Holding the maximum stretch,
roll the eyes up to the crown, stretch
the tongue way out, and growl.

Fig. 3.5 Come to
rest with buttocks on
heels, belly on
thighs, forehead on
mat, palms and
arms forward.

Fig. 3.6 Lift the
buttocks off the heels,
keeping the nose close
to the mat, and shift
toes back into the push
position. Slide elbows,
forearms, and hands
forward and use them
to support the chest's
low forward glide into
the lift.

*Set 3:
Developing Yi*

103

Cobra beginning position. Continue to inhale gently throughout the movement. When the hands have reached their location for the lift, use the forearms and elbows on the mat to support the continued low forward glide of the chest just above the mat. The forward movement extends into the Cobra lifting phase in a continuous motion.

9. **Lower pubic bone to mat, arch the back:** When the chest has come forward to its beginning position, lower the thighs and pubic bone onto the mat. Tighten the buttocks and begin to exhale slowly. Lift with the back and push with the arms to raise into the Cobra. Arch the spine, tuck the chin, and hold; roll the eyes upward, stretch the tongue, and growl.

10. **Repeat:** Repeat the ritual at least two times.

11. **Last round:** Rest on heels, then on back: When you finish the last repetition, relax and collect yourself in the bowed repose on the knees. Then move yourself forward, turn over, and relax fully on your back. Practice conscious breathing as you let your awareness settle on your bodily and energetic sensations.

 ## Basic Cobra's Ritual of Love
Meridians activated: Stomach (yang) and Heart and Lung (yin)

Become comfortable with the details of the Simple Love Cobra so that you can integrate the movements into a smoothly flowing sequence. Examine your experience. The pads of the toes are pressed down onto the mat and the soles of the feet are flexed. This results in a downward push in the toes that is felt as a backward push through the heels. This position gives a good stretch to the muscles, tendons, and ligaments in the toes and the bottoms of the feet, and it stimulates the Kidney 1 Bubbling Springs point. Further, this refreshing stretch engages the Achilles tendon and the gastrocnemius muscles in the backs of the lower legs and extends to the upper legs.

Check your inner connections. When the full Love Cobra is raised to its maximum position, you should feel the push from the toes all the way to the crown. This is achieved by activating the "cobra hood" and by engaging the tongue and the growl, your eyes, and your Yi in combination with the fully connected and completed lift.

An important component of the body's energy is sexual energy. This energy is generated and stored in the lower body near the base of the spine. Indian mystic traditions refer to this life force energy as "serpent power" and the "serpentine force." In yogic circles it is also called kundalini energy. It is

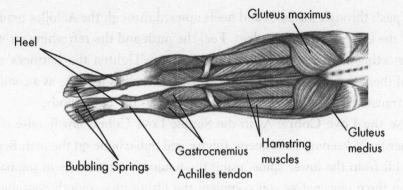

Anatomical view of bottom of feet and back of legs. In practicing the Love Cobra, feel the connective-tissue connection when the toes are pressed down onto the mat, the soles are flexed, and the Achilles tendon and calves are stretched from the heel. Extend that connection to the crown in raised Love Cobra.

Labels: Gluteus maximus, Heel, Gluteus medius, Hamstring muscles, Gastrocnemius, Achilles tendon, Bubbling Springs

described as energy in a dormant state just below the base of the spine, poised like a snake coiled three and a half times. When awakened, kundalini is said to uncoil and forcefully shoot up through the spine into the brain. In his book *Kundalini: The Evolutionary Energy in Man,* Gopi Krishna describes his expansion of consciousness in this way:

> The transformation had been brought about by the vital current that had
> started from below the spine and found access to my brain through the
> backbone. . . . The light I had experienced was internal, an integral part
> of an enlarged consciousness, a part of myself.

This description exemplifies the fact that other cultures and systems, particularly in Asian countries, have long acknowledged the existence of this special inner energy. Its association with serpentine characteristics and the spine is well established. This inner energy awakens the practitioner to another realm of experience within oneself. It may lead to spiritual attainment if properly nurtured.

This sequence of exercises has physical benefits, but the full measure of one's mastery of the "love ritual" will be plumbed in the energy realm.

1. **Begin on belly:** Same as Simple Love Cobra. Lie on your belly with your elbows bent and your palms on the mat. Keep your legs close together, knees no more than about six inches apart. Press the pads of your toes into the mat.

2. **Push from the toes:** Same as Simple Love Cobra. Establish the push from the toes and inhale, and then begin to exhale very slowly. Transfer

the push through the soles and heels upward through the Achilles tendon and the calves in the lower legs. Feel the push and the refreshing stretch connecting the toes through the lower legs. Tighten the buttocks and hold them tight to protect the lower back, as well as to serve as a conduit for transferring force from the toes and legs to the upper body.

3. **Raise the Love Cobra:** As in the Simple Love Cobra, slowly raise your upper body, keeping your knees, thighs, and pubic bone on the mat. Begin the lift from the lower spine, using the tendons and muscles in the back. Keep them engaged as you complete the lifting in a smooth continuous motion by pushing up more with the arms. Sense the transfer of force from the toes through the buttocks as you slowly raise the upper body by pushing up through the hands and arms. As the upper body rises higher, feel the force from the toes rising up, vertebra by vertebra, through the lower spine.

4. **Hold lift:** When you reach the maximum raised position and your spine is fully arched, pause. Stop your breath momentarily and press your tongue to the upper palate (the roof) of your mouth. Feel the connection between the heart and the tongue. Also feel the upward pressure of the tongue connected to and supported by the force of the push coming up through the body from the toes. Tuck the chin in a little more and use your Yi to direct part of the push back to the Jade Pillow, just below the base of the skull. Feel an expansion of pressure, like a hood flaring out at the base of the skull and at the sides and the back of the skull.

5. **Roll eyes up:** Roll the eyes upward in the sockets and focus the force of your mind-eye-heart power, Yi, at the midcrown. Do all these simultaneously: hold your breath; press upward from the toes and the tongue; tuck the chin back; and flare the hood, eyes up and Yi directed to crown. Hold briefly, with not too much pressure.

6. **Release breath, eyes rolled up and tongue out, and gr-r-r-rowl:** Keeping the eyes rolled up and the Yi directed to the crown, stretch the tongue out as far as you can. At the same time, release the breath with a growl. Tightly squeeze your anal and genital sphincter muscles as you growl. After the growl runs out, hold the breath out momentarily and give a little extra contraction to the sphincters. Connect the force to the midcrown using your Yi.

7. **Lower down to the mat:** From this point, the rest of the Basic Cobra's Love Ritual is the same as instructed in the Simple Cobra Ritual. Complete the Basic Cobra Love Ritual, repeating the sequence of movements three times. Then release down to the mat and enjoy the fruits of your practice.

MORE THAN PHYSICAL MECHANICS

Since the cobra is indigenous to Asia and Africa, most North American and European people don't have personal experience with cobras. What are some of the images people have of the cobra's abilities? The following list may serve as a reminder of ideas about the cobra common in folklore and popular culture.

- When Buddha meditated for a long time in the sun, a large king cobra rose up behind him and hovered with its hood expanded out, providing shade for the Buddha.
- Snake charmers in India play music on a reed instrument and a cobra rises up out of a basket and sways as if entranced by the music.
- One type of cobra can project its venom two meters into the eyes of its target, perhaps an enemy or prey.
- Considering its ability to coil and rise up vertically, a cobra can no doubt uncoil with great power to lunge and strike its enemy or prey.

In the wild these talents must indeed be very impressive and attractive to the cobra's prospective mate—not to mention the stimulating effects they likely elicit within the cobra performer. And we have already described the cobra's powerful mating dance. In learning the Cobra's Ritual of Love, create an idealized, humanized image of a cobra embodying the movements in a ritualized performance to woo its paramour.

Keep the mind-eye-heart power, the Yi, engaged. Maintain your feeling awareness in the lower tan tien. Using your imagination, become the cobra in spirit. Feel loving ardor amplified by the aroused hormones of your powerful cobra. Feel the tip of your cobra's tail stabilizing your base and projecting power upward through your body. With chin handsomely tucked, hood regally flared, and tongue impressively stretched way out, release a sexy growl emanating all the way from your cobra's contracted anal and genital sphincter muscles. Keeping your eyes rolled up toward the center of your crown, focused in loving ardor, feel power swell up to the crown from the lower body, strengthened by the cumulative effect of all the upward-directed boosts.

By the time this lovestruck cobra is fully raised in all its glory, the vivifying effects of this exhilarating stretch will be felt from the tips of your toes to the tip of your tongue and the top of your crown. Combined with the force directed upward through the physical connections established in the stretching and arching, the energetic focus on the crown raises vital hormones and energy from the lower body to the head. This benefits the brain and endocrine glands.

Meet Cobie, a Universal Tao instructor's pet white cobra from Thailand. Notice that Cobie is coiled three and a half times. The tip of his tail is coiled in a semicircle in the opposite direction, providing a stabilizing counterforce for the rest of his body. Cobie is glad to meet you—his mouth is open in a big smile and his tongue is extended out in greeting. Admire his lovely flared hood.

Upon completing this phase of expression in the Love Ritual, release the raised pose. With calm dignity, lower your cobra slowly back to the mat. Once your forehead touches the mat, release the feet so that the tops come down on the mat and the soles are relaxed, facing up.

Withdraw your cobra backward to relax and assimilate the effects of its exertions, pleased with its expression of love and ardor. Keeping the hands and forearms on the mat extended in front of your bowed head, move your cobra body back slowly. Keeping the head bowed close to the mat's surface, slide the hands back with the body. Let your torso move back over your thighs until you can rest your buttocks on your heels. Through this deliberate movement the vertebrae in the lower back are flexed gently in the opposite direction from the movement you've just engaged in.

With the buttocks settled on the heels, the head lowers to the mat and the belly and lower chest sink down onto the thighs in repose. The torso relaxes and the spine and chest sink down into comfortable tranquillity, as if melting into the mat (see fig. 3.5). Luxuriate in the pleasant sensations of your body and the peaceful billowing of love energy wafting through your cells.

After a brief meditative rest in conscious breathing, slide the outstretched hands and arms forward to the beginning position. Lift the buttocks from the heels and shift the toes and feet back into the toe-push position. Moving forward, keep your forehead down, the nose just above the mat's surface (see fig. 3.6). Extend into the Cobra lifting phase in one continuous motion. The Cobra's Ritual of Love is repeated at least two more times.

This combination of precisely controlled yang and yin movements and poses is very good for conditioning the physical body. It also facilitates the beneficial distribution of chi and hormones, leaving you with a pleasant feeling of mental equipoise. Both male and female cobras may participate in this ritual. The structures and movements are the same, though the sentiments and imagery may be refined according to one's unique nature. Simply accentuate the positive.

Fancy Cobra's Ritual of Love
Meridians activated: Stomach (yang) and Heart and Lung (yin)

Here are two optional poses that are sometimes nice to add to the movement after the Love Cobra is lowered back down to the mat. These can be done in a manner that maintains the tone and mood of the Cobra's Ritual. They can be performed as slow, sexy spinal undulations that are held briefly in the maximum stretch, to further excite the cobra's paramour.

These poses, called Cat and Droopy Cat, are complementary spinal movements done while supporting the body on the hands and knees. The Cat arches the midspine area, as a cat does when it feels threatened and "puts its back up." The tail and the head are tucked down to achieve a more satisfying stretch over the entire arc of the spine. The Droopy Cat flexes the midspine in the opposite direction while the buttocks and head raise up. After the intensity of stretching the body and arching the spine in the Love Cobra, the Cat provides a stronger balancing stretch for the spine and back.

In the Simple Cobra Ritual, the backward movement of the cobra gently flexes the vertebrae in the lower back in the opposite direction of the movement you just engaged in. However, sometimes the body craves a deeper feeling of balancing relief than the gently flexed vertebrae provide. For this reason we add these paired movements of Cat and Droopy Cat to the Cobra's Love Ritual and *then* move the buttocks back to rest on the heels.

◎ Cat and Droopy Cat

The instructions preceding and following the Cat and Droopy Cat poses are the same as in the Simple Love Ritual and Basic Love Ritual sequences. Add these extra movements just before moving the buttocks back to the heels. The instructions for including the Cat and Droopy Cat follow.

1. **Push back to heels:** Keep the nose close to the surface and push with the forearms, elbows, and palms on the mat to move the body back so that the buttocks finally rest on the feet. Keep the forearms and hands forward on the mat after they finish pushing. Keep the nose close to the mat's surface over the whole distance as the body moves back to the point where the thighs come to a vertical position above the knees.

2. **Lift shoulders and head and arch spine:** At this point stop the movement of the legs, lift the shoulders and head, and continue to slide the hands to a position below the shoulders. Arch the spine up into Cat pose; simultaneously lower the head and tuck the tailbone down to maximize the stretch along the vertebrae. Hold briefly and feel a good stretch.

3. **Release into flexed spine:** Now release the arch of the spine into a deep flexion, lowering into the Droopy Cat pose, the head and buttocks angled upward. Hold for a short time.

4. **Repeat two times:** Repeat these paired spinal stretches twice.

5. **Lower down to mat:** Now slowly bow the head and lower the forearms and elbows down on the mat as the buttocks move back to the heels. When the buttocks settle on the heels, let the belly and lower chest sink down on to the thighs. Lower the forehead to the mat and completely relax the whole torso, feeling as if it were melting into the mat. Enjoy your body sensations and breathe consciously to refresh yourself with energizing golden light.

THE ESSENCE OF RITUAL: INNER FLOWERING

When the steps are followed correctly, a good ritual can at its best create a structure one can learn within. This is particularly true in a "love ritual," the kind of ritual in which emotions and physical sensations urge us to skip steps. Taoists past and present have achieved clear awareness of valuable inner processes and experiences and their beneficial effects. They have passed this knowledge on to others by using teachers in nature, such as the cobra in its love ritual, to demonstrate characteristics of inner dynamics that we should cultivate.

A practitioner can see reflections of these inner dynamics expressed in the Cobra's ritualized structure and movement. The Tao Yin student can gain important insights for adjusting inner alignment and making the right internal connections. In that way the student is enabled (with the help of Yi) to dynamically invoke and energize his or her potential for health, bliss, and evolution. Taoist teachers and forebears have taken the essence of the cobra's ritualistic mating movements and related them to human anatomy in order to identify them for the student's benefit. The anatomies are obviously different but there are functional correspondences: head to head, toes and feet to tail, and the human spine to the upright orientation of the mating cobra. There are nuances in the cobra's actions that correspond energetically to our inner experience. With cobralike movements, practitioners condition the spine and open their energy meridians. They attune themselves to awaken and manipulate the flow of life force energy, chi, in their bodies.

Tremendous potential can be activated by learning to cultivate and coordinate the automatic movement of the interrelated ring muscles throughout the body—the mouth, eyes, anus, perineum, and the urogenital and pelvic diaphragms. Those will, in turn, gradually activate all the involuntary muscles. The heart, veins and arteries are also ring muscles. When this complex of ring muscles is activated, they collectively link with the psoas muscle, establishing inner functional harmony and greatly enhanced power. (This is the goal of Monkey Hugs Knees.) Since the eyes and heart are part of this unified network, one can see a tangible physical base of reality in the body for Yi, the mind-eye-heart power. Activate your Yi and experience the mysterious power of the Cobra.

I hope that some of the descriptions and discussions here have helped you to understand different aspects of the Cobra's Ritual of Love so that you can do it more effectively. Apply the instructions with a positive, patient attitude. Use the elements summarized below in your approach for checking your internalized sense of this and other exercises in the book. Check yourself as you practice the exercises you have already learned. For example, going back over the previous exercises, did you really "get" Monkey Hugs Knees? Did you discover the purpose and catch the spirit? Each exercise has its own benefits; the accumulated skills and power developed through several exercises often combine to provide needed background for the desired results in other movements. All of these exercises have value. Be patient and become your own master.

In learning a new exercise, such as the Cobra's Ritual of Love, it is important to:

1. **Get it right:** Recheck the instructions; the exercise may be different from what you have previously become familiar with.
2. **Discover the purpose:** Try it out. Be aware of what you feel. Feel the connections. Don't automatically fall back on old patterns. Reexamine with inner light and inner feelings. Train your second brain.
3. **Catch the spirit:** Use your imagination to embody the qualities of attitude implied by the exercise's name or that are specified in the instructions. Use your second brain and your Yi!
4. **Be patient:** The essence of ritual is to be patient as you learn the mechanics, the structural aspects of a movement, retraining and reconditioning with full attention. Once the correct mechanics have become second nature and the unique spirit of each exercise is guiding your experience, the chi will flow and your body will glow.
5. **Practice:** The bottom line is "You do it, you get it!"

Become the loving, protective cobra. When you discover that your hood has flared full (energetically it is a clear and distinct feeling), that's good. When your crown and brain become imbued with gentle blissful energy, you're definitely on the right track—you're starting to get it. Keep up the good work. In the next stage, when the bliss blossoms throughout the rest of the body, then you know you've got it! That's a nice welcoming on the inner journey.

Enjoy the rest of the trip. Be like a snake charmer and raise your happy cobra within.

OPENING THE SPINE

All of the following exercises are designed to help you open your spine. Your spine will feel flexible and energized if you do these exercises correctly. Opening the spine will have a beneficial effect on your nervous system—in order to relax you must first relax the spine. These exercises will help the chi to move more freely through the spine and to flow to all the energy centers; they will help your Iron Shirt Chi Kung and Tai Chi practice, too. In terms of health and longevity, keep in mind the saying "You are as young as your spine!"

Begin these movements from your lumbar area, not from your head, neck, or shoulders. Moving from the head, neck, or shoulders is the most common error made by students new to Tao Yin. Remember, the movement begins in the lumbar area (the Door of Life) and gradually moves up the spine and ends with the neck and head.

Because this is a new way for many people to move, it takes concentration to find the correct way to do these exercises. Tucking the chin to lock the neck will help the head to follow, rather than lead, the movement. You may find it helpful to have someone assist you when you are beginning. Have the other person touch your spine to make sure it is straight. Your helper can also gently guide your body to help you learn how to rotate from the lower back.

 ### Peacock Looks at Its Tail
Meridian activated: Spleen (yin)

Before starting this exercise, take a minute to feel your spine. Locate your lumbar area and rotate just the lumbars without moving your neck or shoulders. Put your hands on your lower back and feel the movement you are making. Separate the lumbar area from the rest of your body. Make sure your head and shoulders don't move as you rotate your lumbar area; they should be merely resting atop the lumbar vertebrae and just "going along for the ride," like on a merry-go-round. As a result of the movement at the lumbar spine you should be able to see the ribs moving separately from the pelvis.

As you practice this exercise, think of a peacock. The male peacock is proud of its fanlike plumage, with its many hues and the eyes on the individual plumes. The peacock struts and halts, and with a show of suppleness it slowly turns its neck from the lower part upward, smoothly and section by section, to admire its multi-eyed and multicolored tail. As you practice this movement, be a justly proud peacock moving with regal grace.

1. **Push up, right knee forward:** Begin by lying face down, your palms beside you at midchest. Push through your arms to raise your upper body, then bring the right knee all the way forward on the mat. Adjust your hands so that they line up even with the forward knee (fig. 3.7).

2. **Lower down, move right:** Tuck your chin to lock your neck, which will help you to keep the head, neck, and spine in a straight alignment. Beginning the movement from the lower lumbars, slowly lower the upper body until your abdomen lightly touches your right thigh (fig. 3.8). Remember that your spine should remain straight throughout this movement. Now, keeping the spine straight, initiate a slow sideways movement from the lumbar area. Move the upper body horizontally to the right side above the right thigh. Feel each lumbar vertebrae open.

3. **Twist right:** Begin to slightly twist your lumbars toward the right and upward, one by one. Your hips remain almost parallel to the floor. When the lumbars are fully twisted, rotate the thoracics and then your shoulders (fig. 3.9). Let the neck and head follow until you are able to see your left heel.

    Do not move your head or your upper body first to be able to look at your heel. Keep your spine straight and don't cheat if you can't see the heel. Make your lumbars feel rubbery and soft. Eventually you will become more flexible.

4. **Return to center:** Return to the center position, first turning the lumbars (the tan tien) back to center, then turning the lower thoracics (the solar plexus) back to center, then turning the mid thoracics (the heart center) back to center. Turn the upper thoracics (the throat center) back to center. Finally, turn the cervicals (the mideyebrow) back to center. Then breathe and smile into the back for a couple of breaths.

5. **Repeat:** Repeat the exercise at least twice more on the right side. Remember to maintain your awareness in your lower tan tien so that you train your second brain and also your limbic brain during this reconditioning process.

6. **Switch sides:** Bend the left knee forward and repeat the exercise, this time turning to the left (fig. 3.10).

7. **Return to center:** Come back up to the center position and repeat the movement to the left at least twice more.

Fig. 3.7 From the prone position, lift the upper body by pushing through your arms. Bring the right knee forward.

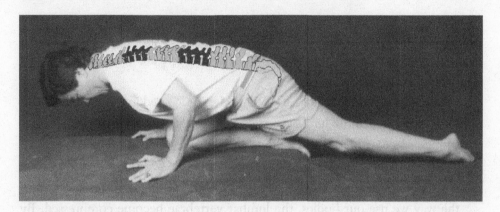

Fig. 3.8 Initiating the movement from the lower lumbars, lower your torso to your thigh. Then move the spine horizontally from the lumbars to the right, above the thigh.

Fig. 3.9 Twist each verebra right and upward, beginning with L4 and L5, then L3, L2, and one by one up through the thoracics and shoulders and finally the neck and head.

Set 3:
Developing Yi

115

Fig. 3.10 Switch to the left side. With the left knee forward, lower the torso to the thigh, move left from the lumbars over the left thigh, then twist left and upward through each vertebra. Finally rotate the shoulders, neck, and head to see the right heel.

8. **Lie on your back:** Relax, smile, and breathe consciously into your spine. If the Peacock was done correctly, the entire spine will feel open and flushed with chi.

   Comment: The Door of Life (Ming Men) is located in the space between the second and third lumbar vertebrae. Taoists regard Ming Men as the storage place of life essence and as a place where chi can enter the body. Your entire upper body—your head, neck, shoulders, arms, ribs, and all your internal organs—rests on the lumbar vertebrae. Because of this weight and the way we use our bodies, the lumbar vertebrae become compressed. By learning how to strengthen the psoas muscle and open the Door of Life, we can avoid joining the ranks of people having surgery on their lower back.

 ## Monkey Rotates Spine to Leg Out
Meridian activated: Bladder (yang)

1. **Begin by sitting:** Sit on the mat with your right leg stretched out in front of you. Bend your left leg, placing the sole of the left foot flat on the inside of your right thigh, the heel near the groin. Place your right hand on the outside of the right leg just above the knee. Put the left hand on the outside of the right leg just below the knee (fig. 3.11).

2. **Bend forward to open Door of Life:** Sitting with the spine erect, tuck your chin and bend forward over your right leg (fig. 3.12). Always start this movement from the lumbar area, keeping your spine straight to open the Door of Life and to stretch the whole spine. Be sure not to lead with your head or upper body. Do not round your back, drop your head, or kiss

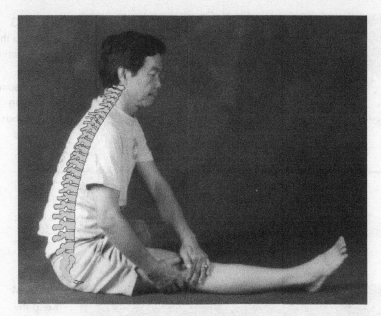

Fig. 3.11
Begin with the right leg stretched and the left knee bent. Both hands are outside the right knee. The spine is straight.

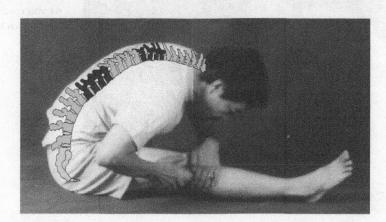

Fig. 3.12
Bend from the lumbars to open the Door of Life, making sure not to strain.

your knee. This movement is intended to facilitate cooperation between the hamstrings and the lumbars. In the beginning you may only be able to move a few inches downward. Go as far as you can without straining.

3. **Rotate right:** After you have come down as far as you can with your spine straight, rotate to the right, starting the twist at the base of the lumbar spine and rotating gradually up the spine, finishing with your neck and head (figs. 3.13 and 3.14). Use your hands on your knee to support the movement. The left hand pulls and the right hand pushes.

Comment: Keep the spine straight as you begin this movement. Your lumbar is the only part of your back that bends forward, then the upper body automatically comes down toward your leg. As you rotate use your

Set 3:
Developing Yi

117

Fig. 3.13
Rotate to the right, starting from the lumbar spine and using your hands to assist the rotation.

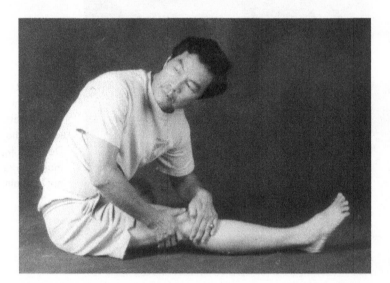

Fig. 3.14
Keep the spine straight as you rotate, then return to center.

hands, pushing and pulling against your leg to add support to the twist. Begin twisting with the lumbars, then the thoracics. Your neck and head are the last parts of your body to move in rotation.

4. **Return to center:** As in the Peacock, return to the center position, first turning the lumbars (the tan tien) back to center, then turning the lower thoracics (the solar plexus) back to center, then turning the mid thoracics (the heart center) back to center. Turn the upper thoracics (the throat center) back to center. Finally, turn the cervicals (the mideyebrow) back to center. Then breathe and smile into the back for a couple of breaths.

5. **Rock side to side:** Gently rock your body side to side from the sitting bones and smile as you breathe into your lumbar region.

6. **Extend hands to midcalf, bend forward to open the Door of Life:** Move your hands down lower on your right leg to the midcalf. With a straight spine, bend forward from your lower lumbars, opening the Door of Life.

7. **Rotate right:** As before, begin rotating slowly to the right, starting the twist at the base of the lumbar spine and rotating gradually up the spine, finishing with your neck and head (fig. 3.15). Use your hands on your knee to support the movement. The left hand pulls and the right hand pushes.

8. **Return to center:** Return to the center position, first turning the lumbars (the tan tien) back to center, then turning the lower thoracics (the solar plexus) back to center, then turning the mid thoracics (the heart center) back to center. Turn the upper thoracics (the throat center) back to center. Finally, turn the cervicals (the mideyebrow) back to center. Then breathe and smile into the back for a couple of breaths.

9. **Extend hands to ankles, bend forward to open the Door of Life:** Move your hands down to your right ankle and foot. With a straight spine, bend forward from your lower lumbar, opening the Door of Life and lengthening the psoas even more. Pull with your hands to stretch the psoas.

10. **Rotate right:** Rotate slowly to the right, beginning with the lower lumbar and then moving gradually up the spine to the head (fig. 3.16).

11. **Return to center:** Complete the upward rotation and return back to the center. Rest and breathe consciously into your spine, feeling the fresh energy moving through your body.

12. **Switch sides:** Switch legs and repeat this sequence on the left side (fig. 3.17).

Fig. 3.15 Move the hands to midcalf and stretch forward, then rotate slowly to the right starting from the lumbars.

Set 3:
Developing Yi

119

Fig. 3.16 Move hands to right ankle and foot and stretch forward, lengthening the psoas muscle even more.

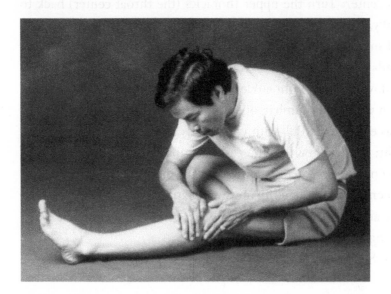

Fig. 3.17 Switch to the left leg and repeat.

 ## Monkey Rotates Spine to Leg In

Monkey Rotates Spine to Leg In is very similar to the previous exercise but it works to increase the flexibility and strength of the hamstring muscles. Be sure to keep the spine straight. Twist from the lumbar spine, making space between the hips and ribs and then between each of the ribs. When you have opened these spaces as much as possible, turn your shoulder and then your head. Many strong tendons that connect to the hip and spine never get an opportunity to move unless you practice consciously turning from the lower lumbar area.

1. **Begin by sitting:** Sit on the mat with your right leg stretched straight out and the left leg bent, the left foot resting flat on the inside of the upper right thigh. If your right hand cannot reach your right ankle, start by holding the knee; hold your left knee with your left hand (fig. 3.18).
2. **Bend forward:** Maintaining a straight spine, lower your upper body from the lower lumbar over the right leg (fig. 3.19).

Fig. 3.18 With the right leg stretched out and the left leg bent, hold the right foot or ankle with the right hand.

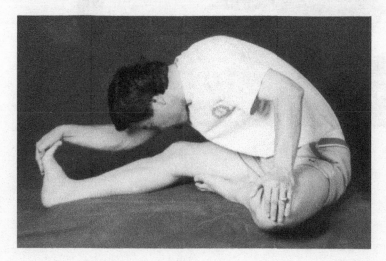

3.19 Bend forward toward the right knee, keeping the spine straight.

3. **Rotate left:** Push your left hand into your knee and begin slowly rotating to the left from the lumbar spine, vertebra by vertebra, until you have turned your whole spine to look up over your left shoulder (fig. 3.20).

4. **Return to center:** As in the Peacock, return to the center position, first turning the lumbars (the tan tien) back to center, then turning the lower thoracics (the solar plexus) back to center, then turning the mid thoracics (the heart center) back to center. Turn the upper thoracics (the throat center) back to center. Finally, turn the cervicals (the mideyebrow) back to center. Then breathe and smile into the back for a couple of breaths.

5. **Repeat:** Repeat a few times.

6. **Shake spine and knees:** Shake your spine and knees slightly and feel the energy moving through your body.

7. **Change sides:** Change sides and repeat the same exercise a few times, turning to the right.

Fig. 3.20
Push the left hand into the knee and rotate the spine to the left.

10

Set 4
Opening Meridians, Removing Abdominal Chi Blockages, Increasing Body Oxygen

The main purpose of several exercises in this chapter is to open meridians in the arms, the legs, or the functional channel. The Empty Force Breath (EFB) practice is introduced to remove stagnant abdominal chi and to greatly increase body oxygen. Besides benefiting the facial skin and preventing "double chin," the Empty Force Breath can be combined with most of the previous Tao Yin exercises to enhance their effectiveness.

Exercises in This Set

1. Monkey Caresses Belly and Arms
2. Monkey Cleans Soles to Crown and Back
3. Monkey Connects Bubbling Springs to Kidneys
4. Rowing a Boat
5. Monkey Arches Back Like Cobra 1, 2, and 3
6. Tao Yin Empty Force Breath Exercises 1, 2, and 3
7. Tiger Resting in Shade
8. Monkey Squatting
9. Snake Peers over Bush
10. Giant Turtle Entering Cave
11. Turtle Emerging from the Sea

The movements in the first four exercises open the yin and yang channels in the arms and legs. It is important to breathe deeply and smile throughout the series.

Monkey Caresses Belly and Arms

Meridians activated: Meridians of the arm—Lung, Pericardium, Heart (all yin); Large Intestine, Triple Warmer, Small Intestine (all yang)

1. **Rub abdomen clockwise in the direction of the large intestine:** The yin channel starts on the abdomen. Begin by rubbing your abdomen with your right hand in a clockwise spiral, circling several times (fig. 4.1). Moving outward in small circles, follow the path of the large intestine up the ascending colon on the right, across the transverse colon, down the descending colon on the left, and back across the lower abdomen.

   Comment: Always spiral clockwise. This helps to move stagnant chi and relieve constipation. However, if you are suffering from diarrhea, the movement should be reversed to counterclockwise to help abate the diarrhea.

2. **Inhale to left shoulder:** After spiralling clockwise around the belly, inhale as you rub your hand up and over your rib cage to the left shoulder (fig. 4.2).

3. **Exhale to rub down inside left arm:** Rotate your arm so that the palm faces up. As you exhale, rub your right hand down the inside of your left arm to the tips of the fingers (fig. 4.3). (The yin channel extends downward.)

4. **Turn palm down and rub up outside left arm:** Now rotate your arm so that the palm faces down. Inhale, rubbing your right hand over the fingertips and up the outside of your left arm, upward over the top of your shoulder (fig. 4.4). (The yang channel extends upward.)

5. **Return to the belly:** Exhale as you bring the right hand back down to the belly. This is a simple and effective way to activate these channels.

6. **Change to left hand and repeat:** With the left hand, rub clockwise circles on your belly several times (fig. 4.5). Inhale, moving your left hand over your ribs on the right side until you reach your shoulder. Now exhale slowly down the inside of your right arm to your fingertips. Turn the right palm down. Inhale as you rub the outside of your arm upward to your shoulder and back to your belly. This completes one round.

7. **Repeat:** Change back to the right hand and repeat at least three times.

For optimum results it is best to practice between eighteen and thirty-six rounds of this exercise. You may find yourself wanting to burp—an important natural result of this exercise—so just let that happen. Swallowing saliva will also enhance the results. This exercise will help alleviate digestive problems. It is good to walk and rub the belly a little after eating to encourage burping. This gives the stomach room for digestion.

Fig. 4.1 Rub your abdomen in a clockwise direction with the right hand.

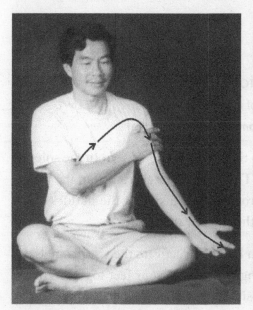

Fig. 4.2 Inhaling, rub the right hand up over the rib cage to the left shoulder before moving down the arm.

Fig. 4.3 Exhaling, rub the right hand down the inside of the left arm to the fingertips.

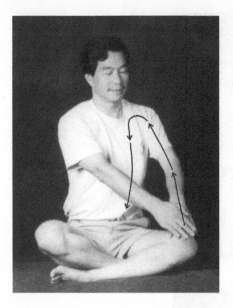

Fig. 4.4 Inhaling, rub the right hand up the outside of the left arm to the shoulder. Then exhale, moving hand to belly.

Fig. 4.5 Rub your abdomen in a clockwise direction with the left hand. Repeat Monkey Caresses Belly and Arms on this side.

 ## Monkey Cleans Soles to Crown and Back

Meridians activated: Meridians of the leg—Spleen, Kidney, and Liver (all yin); Gall Bladder, Bladder, and Stomach (all yang)

The yin meridian channels ascend up the inside of the legs, from the soles of the feet all the way up to the throat. The yang channels run from the throat up over the head, down the back, across to the outside of the buttocks, and down the outside back of the legs to the soles of the feet.

1. **With soles together, rub toes to heels:** To activate the yin channels, sit comfortably on your mat and bring the soles of your feet together. (This is not a stretching exercise; the position of your legs is not as important as sitting comfortably.) Begin by lightly rubbing the soles several times from the toes back to the heels with your fingers and palms (fig. 4.6).
2. **Rub inside ankles and inside lower legs:** When the soles feel relaxed and stimulated, rub up to the insides of the ankles. From there lightly rub up the inside of the lower legs (fig. 4.7); rub up to the groin, abdomen, and chest in a continuous movement (fig. 4.8).

Fig. 4.6 Lightly rub the soles several times from the toes back to the heels.

Fig. 4.7 Once the energy is stimulated in the feet, begin a continuous motion inside the legs toward the upper body.

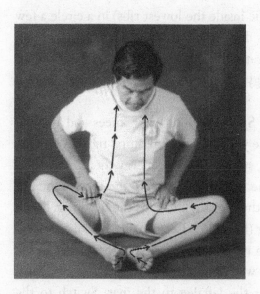

Fig. 4.8 Guide the chi from the inside legs through the groin up the front of the body to the throat.

3. **Continue rubbing upward:** The yang channels start at the throat level. To activate the yang channels at the throat, inhale and bring your hands up over your chin and eyes, over the top of your head, and down over the back of your neck to your shoulders. When you reach your shoulders, bring your hands to the front (since you cannot continue down the back of the shoulders). Trace the hands over the clavicle (the collar bone), around your armpits to the back part of your rib cage, to your kidneys, along the sides of your buttocks, down the outside of your legs to the tops of your feet, and finally to your toes.

4. **Rub feet, exhale up to throat:** Again start rubbing your feet. As you exhale, rub your hands up the inside of your legs and up the front of your body to the rib cage. At throat level, the yang channel begins.

5. **Inhale into yang channels:** Inhale as you bring your hands up over your face, over the top of your head, and all the way down the back and legs to the feet.

6. **Repeat:** Repeat the movement, coming up the front of the body to stimulate the yin channels and down the back and outside of your body, to stimulate the yang channels.

Monkey Connects Bubbling Springs to Kidneys
Meridian activated: Bladder (yang)

1. **With legs outstretched, rub kidneys:** Sit on the mat with your legs stretched out in front of you. Rub the area of your kidneys (on each side of your lower back; the kidneys lie inside the lowest ribs) in a circle a few times. Inhale and rub your hands down the outside of your legs (fig. 4.9); continue over the tops of your feet to the little toes, then to the inside of the soles, guiding kidney energy down the soles of the feet and to Bubbling Springs.

2. **Rub soles, massage Bubbling Springs:** Bend your knees and rub the soles of your feet a few times. Use your thumbs in a spiral motion to massage the Bubbling Spring points, stimulating the energy there.

3. **Grasp toes of left leg:** With the left leg bent, grasp the toes of the left foot. Pull the leg up and stretch the toes back toward the head (fig. 4.10). Now raise and straighten the leg (fig. 4.11). Let your head look up naturally as you raise the foot. Feel a pull from the stretch of the toes in the back of the thigh and calf all the way up to the lower back.

4. **Switch legs and repeat:** Lower the left leg to the mat. Switch to the other leg and repeat, grasping the toes and lifting up. These movements activate the kidneys.

5. **Connect Bubbling Springs to kidneys—rub up inside legs to kidneys:** With both legs back on the mat, exhale as you rub your hands up the inside of your legs to your groin and over the tops of your legs to the kidneys.

6. **Rub kidneys, feel the activated chi:** Rub your kidneys for a moment. The kidney energy has to descend to the soles of your feet in order to activate the water of the Bubbling Springs at the soles. Feel the connection of the activated kidneys' energy with the Bubbling Spring points after you guide it down with your hands.

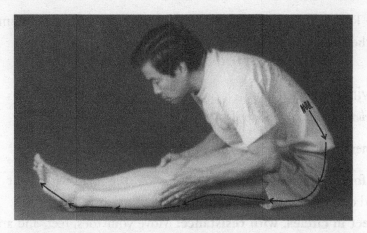

Fig. 4.9 After rubbing the kidneys, move hands down the outside back of the legs, over the little toes, and inside to the soles.

Fig. 4.10 Grasp the toes and prepare to pull them back.

Fig. 4.11 Continue pulling the toes back as you straighten and raise the leg.

7. **Repeat:** Repeat this exercise three to six times, then rest for a moment, feeling the energized response in your body.

Rowing a Boat
Meridian activated: Bladder (yang)

This movement exercises the tendons of the ankles, legs, and back.

1. **Reach forward from lumbars:** Sitting on the mat with your legs stretched out in front of you, reach forward to grasp your toes.
2. **Move feet in circles, with resistance:** Move your toes, feet, and ankles in a circle, circling the left foot clockwise and the right foot counterclockwise, as if you are rowing a boat (fig. 4.12). Offer a little resistance as you move your feet—press forward from the heel as you pull back with the hands, press the feet out at the same time you are pulling them in. Be sure to circle the feet so that all of the tendons are activated.
3. **Reverse:** Now reverse directions, circling each foot and ankle the other way.
    Comment: If you cannot reach your toes easily, drape a cloth underneath the foot. Holding on to both ends of the cloth, circle the foot in both directions. This movement is very good for the tendons at the arches of your feet.
4. **Rest:** Relax and rest for a while, smiling into the tendons on the legs, the spine, and the neck. Feel chi and blood flowing into the tendons. As you relax, picture the tendons growing.

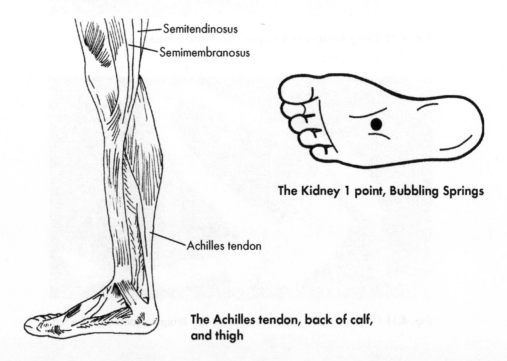

The Kidney 1 point, Bubbling Springs

The Achilles tendon, back of calf, and thigh

Fig. 4.12 Grasping the toes, circle the feet: the left foot circles clockwise and the right foot circles counterclockwise.

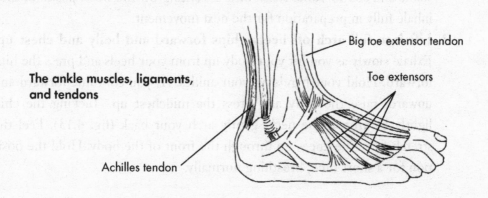

Big toe extensor tendon

Toe extensors

The ankle muscles, ligaments, and tendons

Achilles tendon

 ## Monkey Arches Back Like Cobra

Meridian activated: Stomach (yang)

◐ Part 1: Lift from Mat

1. **Sit on feet, lean back, stretch thighs:** Kneel on the mat with your knees about six inches apart. Sit your buttocks on your feet. Now lean back, placing your hands on the mat behind you, fingers pointing back or a bit outward. As you exhale, slightly lift your belly up toward the ceiling, arching your back gently. This position stretches the top of the thigh muscles. Don't go too far. Stretch within your comfort zone and breathe to your thigh muscles.

2. **Lift and release down:** Lift the belly slightly and then bring it back down, leaving your hands behind you on the mat.

3. **Repeat:** Repeat this movement several times. When you have come to feel comfortable with Part 1, you can use it as a warm-up and then proceed to Part 2. If you are just beginning your studies of Tao Yin, you may want to take a few weeks practicing Part 1 before moving on to Part 2.

◎ Part 2: Lift from Raised Heels

1. **Sit on raised heels:** Kneel on the mat with the feet together and the knees about six inches apart. Press the pads of the toes into the mat and raise the heels up. Reach back with the left hand and grasp the left ankle/heel, then grasp the right ankle/heel with the right hand. Straightening your arms to support yourself, sit back on your heels. Adjust your body so that you feel stable and comfortable. Relax into the sitting-on-the-heels position, then inhale fully in preparation for the next movement.

2. **Lift into full arch off heels—hips forward and belly and chest up:** Exhale slowly as you lift your body up from your heels and press the hips forward. Hold your hands on your ankles. As you continue forward and upward, raise the belly and press the midchest up. Tucking the chin lightly to protect the neck, gently arch your back (fig. 4.13). Feel the stretch from the knees up through the front of the body. Hold the position for a short time, breathing normally.

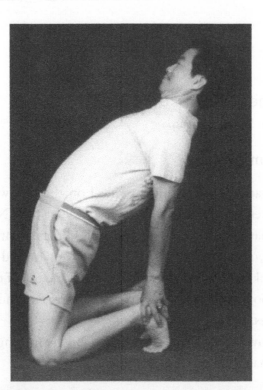

Fig. 4.13 Reach back to grasp ankles/heels. Press hips forward, raise the belly and chest, and arch back with your chin tucked.

3. **Release back to heels:** Release the upward position and, keeping your hands on your ankles, relax yourself back to sit on your raised heels. Rest.

4. **Repeat:** Repeat this movement a few times.

5. **Finish on back:** Finish by resting on your back, inhaling golden light to the affected areas and exhaling the cloudy gray energy. When you feel comfortable and proficient in performing this arching exercise from the raised heels position, advance to Part 3.

⊙ Part 3: Lift From Knees

1. **Kneeling, support your back:** Kneel with your knees about six inches apart, your feet angled inward and your toes pointed back, flat on the mat. Place your hands on your lower back or hips to support your lower back. Inhale.

2. **Arch up, bend back:** As you exhale, push your buttocks forward and up as you arch your spine, the chin lightly tucked (fig. 4.14). Steady yourself with your arms on the back of your hips and breathe normally.

3. **Grasp upturned heels:** Slowly reach back with the left hand and grasp your left foot, placing your palm on the heel with the fingers on the inside of the ankle and the thumb on the outside. Do the same on the right side, arching back as you shift to this position. (Later, when you feel

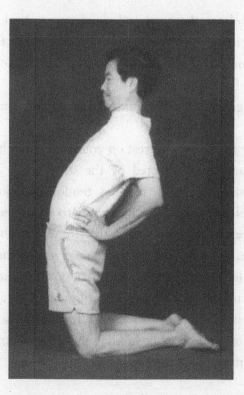

Fig. 4.14 With your hands on your lower back, push your buttocks forward and up.

Fig. 4.15 Press hips and pelvis forward and up.

more confident with this arch position, you can grasp your feet with fingers on the outside of the ankles.)

4. **Move into full arch:** Firmly holding your heels or ankles, slowly press your hips and pelvis forward and up, keeping your spine comfortably arched and your chin slightly tucked (fig. 4.15). Feel the stretch along the front of your thighs and upper body. Hold the stretch for a short time and breathe into it.

5. **Release to knees:** Release the arch and slowly come back up to the kneeling position, placing your hands on the backs of the hips for support. Once you have returned to the kneeling position, lower your buttocks back to sit on the feet for a brief rest.

6. **Repeat:** Return to beginning position and repeat this movement at least two times.

7. **Finish on back:** After the last round rest on your back, breathing golden light into the spine and areas affected by the stretch. As you exhale, release toxins and tension held in the muscles, tendons, and joints.

8. **Advanced option—release the full arch directly to sit on feet:** The following is an alternative method of releasing the stretch for when you feel stronger, more flexible, and more confident. You can release the stretch by arching the spine and lowering your buttocks back down toward your feet while still holding the ankles. Support yourself with your arms as you move back to sit on your feet. Relax and rest briefly. Repeat the stretch twice more by arching up into position while holding the ankles from the sitting position. Support the movement as necessary with the arms.

TAO YIN EMPTY FORCE BREATH

This breathing method is being introduced at this point because you've now had time to gain a sense of ease and familiarity with the exercises. You can add this complementary practice to your routine by selecting which exercises to use it with. There are also some new exercises introduced in this section.

The Tao Yin Empty Force Breath is a Chi Kung breathing method used to increase the oxygen available in the body. Every cell in the body, about seventy-five trillion of them, needs oxygen to maintain health and proper functioning. The Empty Force Breath is an extension of the normal exhalation. It can be performed by itself by fully exhaling, emptying the air out of the body, and then holding the breath out. It is completed by drawing the organs up into the dome of the rib cage and then expanding them back down consciously, repeating this up-and-down movement a few times before inhaling. This manner of exhaling creates a strong vacuum suction in the abdomen. The abdominal vacuum can draw air directly into the digestive tract to oxygenate the blood, thereby enhancing the level of overall body functioning. Empty Force Breath can also be combined with other exercises to increase their effectiveness.

Caution: People with heart problems or uncontrolled high blood pressure should proceed very carefully. Consult your doctor if you have a concern about your condition.

The Empty Force Breath (EFB) has been adapted for the Tao Yin exercises. It enables the blood to carry greatly increased quantities of oxygen more quickly to the muscles and tendons in the areas of the body targeted by a given exercise. Along with the nutrients in the blood and the energizing chi that is directed by the breath, the increased oxygen in the blood acquired via the Empty Force Breath produces more powerful results in Tao Yin practice.

This process of delivering increased amounts of oxygen into the blood has been used in the Taoist breatharian practices for a few thousand years. Western science has recently discovered that the digestive tract is lined with the same kind of oxygen-absorbing cells as the lungs, enabling the intestines to absorb oxygen directly into the bloodstream. More than just being able to deliver a supplemental reserve of oxygen, the Empty Force Breath greatly increases the amount of oxygen available for immediate use in areas of the lower body. Oxygen coming from the lungs has to be transferred from the lungs to the heart first, before being delivered to the lower body. Oxygen takes more time to get to the lower body from the lungs than from a freshly charged supply in the intestines.

As well, the intestines can deliver more oxygen to the affected area in the lower body—a larger volume of air can be retained after being inhaled directly into the digestive tract and into the intestines than can be processed by the lungs. The reason that the intestines can deliver more oxygen to the blood is that the surface area for the twenty-eight to thirty feet of the intestines can absorb five, ten, twenty, to possibly fifty times more oxygen than the lungs can. Of course, these numbers are arbitrary. The degree of success would depend on the condition and cleanliness of the intestines, as well as on one's proficiency in doing the Empty Force Breath practice.

The oxygenation that can be achieved for the body under these favorable conditions is a tremendous improvement over normal breathing. Normally when one breathes through the nose the volume of air intake is greatly restricted due to the small size of the nostril passageway. Further, much of the inhaled air is exhaled, along with the used gases such as carbon dioxide. The oxygen delivered through the Empty Force Breath, on the other hand, is retained in the digestive tract. (You must be breathing good-quality air for

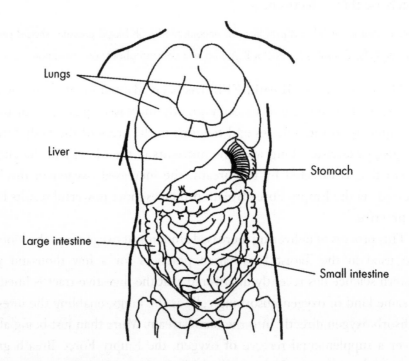

The large and small intestines. Lined with the same kind of cells for absorbing oxygen as the lungs, the large and small intestines provide a much greater surface area for oxygen absorption. The lining of the stomach and the esophagus also have this capacity for oxygen absorption.

this practice to be of maximum benefit.) Eventually, after most of the oxygen has been absorbed and transferred to the blood, the unusable retained air would be released in the normal way—most likely down and out, as gas, but also up and out, through the lungs.

The Empty Force Breath practice should only be done on an empty stomach. The breath practice involves emptying the air out of the lungs, holding the breath out, performing the Tao Yin exercise, and then "gasping" air directly into the digestive tract. Air will also enter the lungs at this time. With the breath held out, the diaphragm, organs, and muscles of the abdomen can be exercised.

One basic Empty Force Breath practice is to squeeze the abdominal organs using internal power, so as to reduce the space that the organs occupy. At the same time, inwardly draw the organs back toward the spine. The next step is to "suck" the organs up into the lower rib cage by means of the thoracic diaphragm. (This is done without taking in supplemental external breath.) You then press the organs down and expand them outward toward the front. Then you squeeze them into a compact volume again and draw them in toward the spine, and finally you suck them back up into the rib cage without breathing. This procedure helps to create a strong vacuum suction, an "empty force."

This pattern constitutes one cycle; you can visualize it as rolling a ball in a circle. This particular breath practice can be performed sitting, standing, or in any position in which abdominal movement is possible.

Empty Force Breath Exercises

Begin by sitting in a comfortable cross-legged position on the mat. Place your hands on the hips with the fingers to the front and thumbs to the back to support your movements in the exercise.

Exercise 1: Rounded Mouth

The Rounded Mouth exercise is combined with the practice Rolling the Ball. This exercise will activate the facial muscles and bring more oxygen to the face. Regular practice will help get rid of facial wrinkles.

Because these exercises have you holding your breath out, take two preparatory breaths before beginning, to provide extra oxygenation. This extra oxygen will make holding the breath out more comfortable.

1. **Preparatory inhalation:** First exhale to clear the lungs. Then, with mouth closed, briskly suck in a strong, deep breath through the nose into the lungs. Hold for a short, comfortable time to enhance oxygen absorption in the lungs by locking the throat with a chin tuck (fig. 4.16).

2. **Release breath:** Untuck the chin and empty the lungs by blowing a long, relaxed, and steady exhale out of the mouth (fig. 4.17).

3. **Second inhalation:** Inhale as in step 1: With the mouth closed, briskly suck in a strong, deep breath through the nose to fill the lungs. Tuck the chin, holding a little longer this time to increase oxygen absorption. Exhale again by blowing out through the mouth.

4. **"Cho-o-o-o-o" release:** Inhale a third time, increasing the hold time to a little longer still. When you are ready, forcefully release the held breath making the "Cho-o-o-o-o" sound. Continue the exhalation with the mouth open wide (fig. 4.18). You may also extend the tongue out for a more powerful effect. As you exhale, use your diaphragm to forcefully compact the large lower lobes of the lungs upward. At the same time use all the muscles around the heart and lungs to fully compress the lungs. Remember to stay within your comfort zone.

   Squeeze the abdominal organs and flatten the abdomen toward the back. Firmly contract the urogenital and anal sphincter muscles so that you can feel the force of the "Cho-o-o-o-o" sound coming from deep in the body, not just from the top of the chest and throat. The sound should have a wheezing quality that emits from deep in the lungs. Squeeze out all of the air that you can.

   Holding the breath out, internally suck the thoracic diaphragm as high as possible inside the rib cage to create the maximum empty force.

5. **Round mouth, extend tongue, roll eyes up:** With the diaphragm sucked up high inside the rib cage and with the lungs emptied, round the lips over the teeth, making an O shape around the mouth. (Don't open the jaws too wide.) Extend the tongue out with power through the rounded mouth and roll the eyes up toward the crown (fig. 4.19).

6. **Rolling the ball:** Keeping the lungs emptied out and the mouth, tongue, and eyes engaged, exercise the diaphragm, organs, and abdominal muscles by practicing Rolling the Ball:

   1. At the end of the "Cho-o-o-o-o" exhalation, imagine drawing a ball up to the very top of the dome formed by the fully raised diaphragm.

   2. Without inhaling, roll the ball down below the rib cage by pressing the diaphragm down as far as it can go.

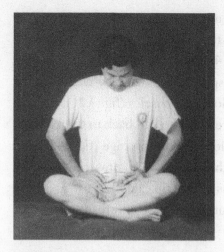

Fig. 4.16 Suck in a deep breath through the nose, hold the breath, and tuck the chin.

Fig. 4.17 Untuck the chin and release the breath in a long, steady exhale.

Fig. 4.18 Forcefully release the breath with the "Cho-o-o-o-o" sound, mouth open wide. Suck the diaphragm high up into the rib cage, fully emptying the lungs.

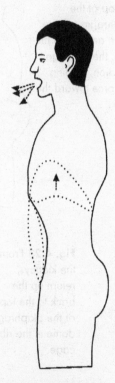

Fig. 4.19 Holding the breath out, round the mouth, extend the tongue, and roll the eyes upward.

Directing the forces of the "Cho-o-o-o-o" exhale. Flatten the abdomen toward the spine, contract the diaphragm upward in the dome of the rib cage.

Set 4: Opening Meridians

3. Maintaining the continuity of movement by using your Yi synchronized with your abdominal muscles, push the ball farther down and out to the front as far as the belly will go (fig. 4.20).

4. Next, roll the ball in toward the spine in the back by changing the direction of force of the lower abdominal muscles (fig. 4.21).

5. When the belly is flattened and pressing the ball back to the kidneys, roll the ball up the back into the dome of the rib cage (figs. 4.22 and 4.23). Use the Empty Force "breathless suction" to draw the ball back up to the top of the raised dome inside the rib cage. You can assist the pull up by extending the tongue out further as you (breathlessly) suck the ball up.

Fig. 4.20 To begin Rolling the Ball, direct the forces from the top of the diaphragm's dome down and out to the front, then change direction, guiding the force toward the back.

Fig. 4.21 Roll the ball back toward spine.

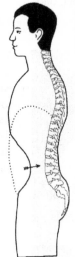

Fig. 4.22 Press the ball against kidneys.

Fig. 4.23 From the kidneys, return up the back to the top of the diaphragm dome in the rib cage.

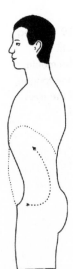

Fig. 4.24 Finish Rolling the Ball by gasping air into the intestines. Release the ball, the tongue, and the eyes.

6. Repeat Rolling the Ball several times, as long as you can comfortably hold the breath out.

   Comment: Besides massaging the organs, exercising the abdominal muscles, and moving stagnant chi, Rolling the Ball creates the conditions for a strong vacuum to suck air that will be gasped directly into the whole digestive tract.

7. Gasp air down to the esophagus, stomach, and intestines: When you need to breathe again, press the diaphragm and abdominal organs downward, open your mouth, and quickly expand your compressed abdomen to the front, back, sides, up, and down simultaneously. This will create the strong vacuum suction. The vacuum that you create sucks air down the esophagus through the stomach into the small intestine and finally into the large intestine (and also into the lungs) (fig. 4.24). The rush of air sucked in by the abdominal vacuum causes a gasping sound as the air passes through the throat.

   Before exhaling, swallow down forcefully, then lock the neck and use your Yi to push the air down through the esophagus and stomach to the intestines in order to retain the air in the digestive tract. At first, more air will bypass the lungs as the strong vacuum suction draws it into the digestive tract. After the initial rush of air, the lungs will fill up more.

8. Repeat: Do the exercise ten times, or fewer as necessary to stay in your comfort zone.

⊙ Exercise 2: Jutting Jaw

The Jutting Jaw exercise is done to tighten the skin of the throat and under the chin, preventing "double chin."

1. **Forcefully jut your lower jaw outward:** Following the instructions for the Rounded Mouth exercise just described, after step 4 (the "Cho-o-o-o-o" release) bare your lower teeth, jut the lower jaw forward forcefully, and hold it (fig. 4.25). You do this instead of rounding the mouth and sticking the tongue out. Feel the skin being stretched under the chin and in the throat area.

2. **Roll eyes up:** Roll the eyes up toward the crown. Maintain the jutted jaw with bared teeth and eyes rolled up (fig. 4.26).

3. **Combine Jutted Jaw with Rolling the Ball:** Continue with Rolling the Ball as described in step 6 above.

4. **Repeat:** Repeat this combined sequence ten times.

These two exercises (Rolling the Ball and Jutting Jaw) may be performed sitting on raised heels or kneeling (figs. 4.27 and 4.28). These positions afford a somewhat more powerful execution of the exercises. Sitting on raised heels especially increases the internal power of the diaphragm and the abdominal pull-up. You can practice Rolling the Ball in this position or in the kneeling position. Experiment by changing between cross-legged, on raised heels, and kneeling positions from time to time as you do repetitions of the exercises.

Fig. 4.25 Jut the lower jaw out forcefully.

Fig. 4.26 Hold the jaw forward, baring the teeth and rolling the eyes.

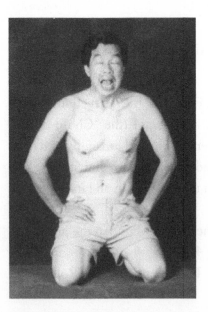

Fig. 4.27 The "Cho-o-o-o-o" exhalation on raised heels.

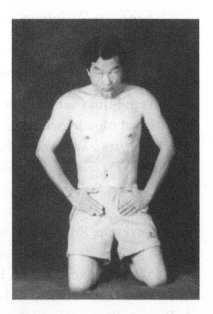

Fig. 4.28 Rounded Mouth and Rolling the Ball in kneeling.

✺ Exercise 3: Refined Abdominal Rolling

For further benefit you can refine the "rolling" process by developing control of muscle groups in specific areas. Work on a section at a time with each Empty Force Breath. With each successive breath move to the next area.

1. **Middle sector, left side, right side of abdomen:** Start by practicing Rolling the Ball in the middle sector of the abdomen, then on the left side, then switch to the right side. Once you have gained some facility with these large sectors, work within the middle sector and do some mini-rolls.

2. **Middle sector mini-rolls:** Begin Rolling the Ball in a smaller circle within the lower abdomen, then move up to the middle abdomen, then the upper abdomen, and finally in the lower rib cage on successive Empty Force Breaths.

   Comment: Blood, chi, and oxygen are directed to areas affected by the exercises. The abdominal area receives the benefit of a greatly increased availability of oxygen as a result of the Empty Force Breath and the abdominal exercises. Oxygen is necessary for metabolizing fat. The increased oxygen from these exercises will help burn off excess body fat. Do more abdominal rolling exercises to remove excess fat in the belly area.

   By developing greater awareness and control of the different muscle groups in this important area you also become enabled to more effectively direct the internal force and chi. Among the many applications of this ability, you can greatly strengthen your grounding connection to the earth as developed in Chi Kung practice. The grace and power of one's Tai Chi practice is greatly enhanced when the movements are directed from the tan tien.

✺ Empty Force Breath Combined with Tao Yin

To use the Empty Force Breath in combination with a Tao Yin exercise, get into the beginning position of that particular exercise. Normally you would inhale in the beginning position and then begin the active movement on the exhale. With the Empty Force Breath added to an exercise, do the preparatory breaths for the Empty Force Breath as previously instructed. Begin moving into the position as you exhale the "Cho-o-o-o-o" sound.

If moving to the full position while exhaling like this is not possible, do the "Cho-o-o-o-o" exhale first, take an extra breath, and then exhale as you assume the full Tao Yin position. Empty your lungs as best you can, then hold your breath out and do some form of Empty Force diaphragm and abdominal

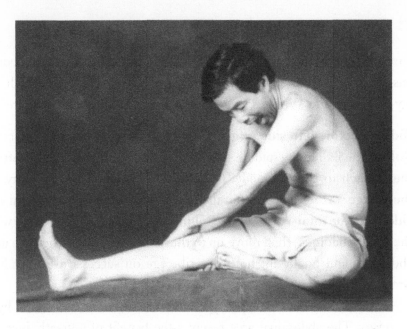

Using the Empty Force Breath, move into the Tao Yin position with the "Cho-o-o-o-o" exhalation. Here Master Chia uses the "Cho-o-o-o-o" exhalation in Monkey Rotates Spine to Leg Out.

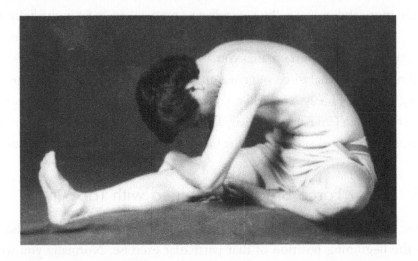

The Empty Force Breath in a full Tao Yin position: Rolling the Ball in Monkey Rotates Spine to Leg Out.

movement. Smile with your lips closed. It is not necessary to stick the tongue out during the Empty Force out-breath exercise, but do it when you feel inspired to.

EMPTY FORCE BREATH OPTIONS
FOR TAO YIN EXERCISE

Choose a Tao Yin exercise or sequence within an exercise that lends itself to being able to practice some form of Empty Force diaphragm and abdominal movement. You might choose one of the following Empty Force Breath exercises to fit the particular Tao Yin movement.

1. **Roll the Ball in the basic circular pattern:** You may do this when the abdominal muscles are not tensed in the Tao Yin position and a full range of abdominal movement is possible.

2. **Use Empty Force Breath suction to raise the diaphragm up and then press it down repeatedly:** If there is light tension, it may be possible to only do this simple repetitive up-and-down movement. Repeat the up-and-down movement as long as is comfortable.

3. **When no abdominal movement is possible, suck the diaphragm up and hold:** In this situation, hold your exhalation out and use breathless suction to suck the diaphragm up into the ribcage, holding the diaphragm there until you're ready to breathe.

4. **Conclude and release from the Empty Force Breath exercise:** When you are in a Tao Yin pose and want to release from the Empty Force Breath exercise:
   1. Press the diaphragm and organs downward and expand them.
   2. Simply let the vacuum thus created suck the air down through the throat with the gasping sound and swallow hard to retain it. Then move on to the next phase of the Tao Yin sequence, perhaps the resting position.
   3. Relax and breathe as in a normal Tao Yin resting phase.

Food is normally aerated and mixed with saliva during mastication (chewing). With greatly increased oxygen in the blood and available to the intestines, digestion can be more effective and more efficient. Since about 80 percent of the body's normal supply of oxygen is used by the brain, the groggy feeling after eating can be eliminated. Thus mental alertness can function unimpaired after meals, especially if you do not overeat.

Certainly it is best to do Empty Force breathing before meals, rather than soon after a meal!

Tiger Resting in Shade

This is the first exercise of the sitting positions. It is important to become comfortable in a variety of postures when working on the mat.

1. **Sit with knees bent:** Sit on the mat with knees bent, hands touching the mat on each side of you. Let your legs fall to the right side. Hold each lower leg with your hand (fig. 4.29).
2. **Practice:** Practice sitting in this position for one to two minutes. Feel your sitting bones making contact with the ground. Feel the back straight and lifted to the sky.
3. **Legs to center:** Bring both legs back to center.
4. **Repeat:** Repeat this sitting exercise on the left side.

 ## Monkey Squatting

Meridians activated: Bladder (yang) and Kidney (yin)

1. **Squat:** Squat down with your heels flat on the floor, arms inside the knees and fingers interlaced (fig. 4.30). Bounce a little bit, shifting your weight from side to side.
2. **Practice:** This posture opens the hips and releases tension in the lower back. You can practice this posture when eating, reading, or meditating.

Fig. 4.29 Let the legs fall to the right side, right hand holding right ankle, left hand holding left calf. The back is straight.

Fig. 4.30 Squat with heels flat on the floor and bounce.

Snake Peers over Bush

1. **Wrap arm around knees and rock:** Sit on the floor. Bring your knees up to the chest and wrap your arms around them (fig. 4.31). Rock back and forth a little bit.

2. **Practice:** Feel the hips open and the spine lengthen.

    Comment: It is important to sit in a variety of different postures. Many problems in the West come from sitting only in chairs. Try sitting on the floor when you eat, read, or watch television. Bring these sitting postures into your daily life.

Fig. 4.31 Bring knees up to the chest, wrap the arms around the knees, and rock back and forth.

 ## Giant Turtle Entering Cave

Meridians activated: Meridians of the leg—
Spleen, Kidney, Liver (all yin); Bladder (yang)

The turtle is renowned in Chinese medicine for its long life. The turtle's longevity is due to the openness of the Functional Channel. This Tao Yin movement facilitates the opening of the Functional Channel. You can use the Empty Force Breath in the forward position.

1. **Soles together, bend forward:** Sitting with your feet in front of you, bring the soles together and hold your feet with both hands (fig. 4.32). Bend forward and down from your lower back, rounding your back slightly as you move forward (fig. 4.33). Tuck the chin toward the chest as you bend the upper body down toward the mat.

2. **Stretch neck:** Next, moving only from your neck, inhale, stretch, and look up, bringing your head back slightly (fig. 4.34).

3. **Straighten spine:** Straighten the spine and return to the beginning position. Be careful not to overstretch.

Fig. 4.32 Bring the soles of the feet together and hold with both hands.

Fig. 4.33 Bend forward from the lumbar spine, rounding the back. The chin is tucked.

Fig. 4.34 Moving only from your neck, stretch and look up.

4. **Move like a turtle:** Bend forward on an exhale, back straight. (You may bend a little bit toward the floor by lowering your head and rounding your upper back and stretching your chin toward the chest.)
5. **Stretch neck:** Inhale as you stretch your neck and look up.
6. **Straighten spine:** Straighten the spine, returning to the beginning position. Feel as if you are making a circle with your chin, like a turtle does. Swallow your saliva.
7. **Rock:** Rock yourself a little bit and shake your knees.

Comment: Swallowing the saliva is a secret teaching. Taoists refer to the esophagus as being twelve stories high, a reference to the valves in the esophagus that only allow food to go down, not up. Normally when you swallow your saliva it travels down the esophagus and sits on the closed valve until there is enough saliva to continue going down through the valve. But according to Taoist teachings, when the saliva sits there it blocks energy and turns into mucus. Therefore, learn to swallow correctly:

1. To swallow your saliva correctly, lock your chin and raise the crown to make the throat tight.
2. Inhale, hold your breath, and make the throat tight so that it is hard to swallow.
3. Prepare the saliva and swallow hard, making a forceful gulping sound. Push the saliva hard down the throat, using your Yi. Feel it pass through the esophagus and down through the stomach to the small intestine and into the area of the lower tan tien. The tan tien fire will burn and transform it to chi.

Using this practice, you actually force the saliva down with chi pressure. Swallowing "nectar" in this manner provokes burping, allowing gas that is stuck in your stomach to escape. You'll find saliva swallowing to be an effective way to promote healthy belching.

Turtle Emerging from the Sea
Meridians activated: Meridians of the leg—
Spleen, Kidney, Liver (all yin); Bladder (yang)

1. **Sit with soles together:** Sit with your feet in front of you. Put your soles together and hold the feet with your hands (fig. 4.35).
2. **Bend forward:** Starting from the lower back, move your upper body toward the floor.

3. **Rotate right:** Now rotate to the right, beginning the rotation from the lower back and eventually rotating through the midback. Turn and gently look over your right shoulder, rotating your neck slightly (fig. 4.36).

4. **Return to center:** Return to face the center, inhale, and relax.

5. **Rotate left:** Now do the same movement on the left side (fig. 4.37), then return to center.

6. **Repeat:** Repeat a few times and rock yourself a little bit.

Fig. 4.35 Hold the soles of the feet together with your hands.

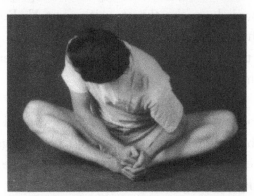

Fig. 4.36 Rotate right starting with the lumbars. Look over the right shoulder.

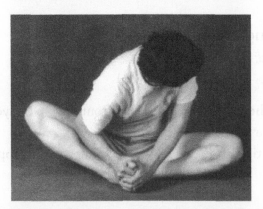

Fig. 4.37 Repeat the movement rotating to the left.

Tao Yin
Exercises
150

11

Set 5

The Straight Vector in the Curve—
Stretching and Growing the
Tendons

The emphasis in this set of exercises is on growing, strengthening, and enhancing the elasticity of the tendons in the torso and arms. When you spiral and twist the fingers, wrist, and elbow, the tendons curve around the bones. If you hold this curve by maintaining a series of counterforces while attempting to straighten the arm, the tendons stretch. Stretching the tendons of the arms in this way will extend the connection from the arms to the neck, the spine, the lower back, and all the way down to the legs. This chapter also includes conditioning exercises for the spine. All of the exercises begin in a cross-legged sitting position on the mat.

Exercises in This Set

1. Pheasant Opens Its Wings
2. Dragon Stretches Tail and Claws to Side
3. Dragon Stretches Tail and Claws Up
4. Dragon Stretches Tail and Claws to Both Sides
5. Dragon Stretches Tail and Claws to Front
6. Pull Bow and Shoot the Arrow
7. Bamboo Swinging in the Wind
8. Turn and Open the Door of Life
9. Hummingbird
10. Bear Stretches Its Back

11. Snake Coils around Tree
12. Swimming Dragon

 ## Pheasant Opens Its Wings

The main theory of Pheasant Opens Its Wings and the preparation exercises that precede it can be summed up in the saying, "Find the straight vector in the curve." Tendons in the spine, neck, and legs connect and integrate when you twist from the arms correctly. In the resting period, smile to the tendons and feel chi and blood flow to them. Feel them grow and become stronger.

Preparation Exercise: Thumb Counterforce Twist

These preparatory exercises activate balanced counterforces in the arms and help you to experience the stretching of the tendons.

1. **Twist thumb and fingers left and feel counterforce:** Sitting cross-legged on the mat, grab the right wrist with your left hand with moderate firmness. Twist the thumb to the left (clockwise) and let the fingers and palm follow as far as they can. Hold the wrist and feel the counterforce as the thumb, palm, and fingers turn in one direction while the wrist turns in the opposite direction (fig. 5.1).

Fig. 5.1 The thumb, palm, and fingers turn in one direction while you turn the wrist in the opposite direction.

2. **Release, then repeat:** Release, then hold and twist again. Repeat this exercise a few times so that the tan tien brain and the limbic brain become fully aware of the internal structure of the counterforces.

3. **Create the counteracting forces without holding:** This time create the counteracting forces without holding the wrist. Use your Yi, your mind-eye-heart power, to twist the hand while holding the wrist in balanced opposition.

4. **Elbow counterforces—pull elbow in with right hand:** Maintain the counterforces you established with the thumb and wrist twist. Notice the natural tendency of the elbow to move out away from your body as you turn your hand. Now hold your right elbow with your left hand and lightly pull the elbow in with the hand. Simultaneously push the right elbow out lightly, creating a balance of the counterforces. Continue this counterforce twisting of hand, wrist, and elbow so that you feel the tendons wrapping around the bones. As you continue the counterforce twisting, focus your Yi so that it is extended from wrist to elbow to shoulder all the way to the scapula.

5. **Repeat with the left arm:** Begin by twisting the thumb to the right (counterclockwise) and let the fingers and palm try to follow.

◑ *Preparation Exercise: Little Finger Counterforce Twist*

1. **Twist the little finger and palm left and feel counterforce:** Grasp the right wrist with the left hand. Begin by twisting the little finger counterclockwise (to the front and around toward the left) letting the fingers, thumb, and palm follow while the left-hand grip opposes the movement (fig. 5.2). Feel the counterforces as the right hand tries to turn while the left hand opposes the movement. Do this a few times: tense, feel the counterforces, and release.

2. **Find the same counterforces without holding the right wrist:** This time use your mind-eye-heart power to find those counterforces in the same movement.

3. **Push elbow out with right hand:** Notice that your elbow tends to move inward toward your body with this hand movement. This time hold the inside of your right elbow with your left hand. Let the left hand lightly push the elbow out, creating a balance of counterforces (fig. 5.3). Do this several times to register the feeling of the inner structure of the balanced counterforces.

4. **Continue counterforce twisting:** Remove the left hand from the elbow and maintain the counterforces you established with the pinky finger twist

Fig. 5.2 Twist the pinky finger counter-clockwise. Hold the right wrist with the left hand, opposing the movement.

Fig. 5.3 The left hand lightly pushes the elbow out, creating a balance of counterforces.

and the wrist countertwist. Continue this counterforce twisting of hand, wrist, and elbow so that you feel the tendons wrapping around the bones. Feel the balance of counterforces from the hand to the wrist, to the elbow, and to the shoulder and scapula.

5. **Do the same exercises with the left arm:** Begin by twisting the little finger clockwise (to the front and around toward the right) with the fingers, thumb, and palm trying to follow.

Pheasant Opens Its Wings

Meridians activated: Meridians of the arm—Lung, Pericardium, Heart (all yin); Large Intestine, Triple Warmer, Small Intestine (all yang)

Now you're ready to practice the movement Pheasant Opens Its Wings. As usual, stay within your comfort zone. Don't stretch too forcefully; build your strength and elasticity in your tendons stage by stage. First get the feel for how to "set the curve" (wrap tendons around bone) and "find the straight vector" (stretch them more) in a slow, rhythmic motion. Then coordinate your breath with the movement: inhale while setting up the curve and exhale while finding the straight vector inside the curve.

1. **Spiral fingers in toward chest:** Sitting cross-legged with your head erect and your back comfortably straight, extend your arms out in front of you at shoulder height, palms facing each other. Spiral your fingers upward and inward, starting with the little finger and letting each of the other fingers follow in succession, until the fingers point to your chest (fig. 5.4). The palms will naturally turn upward and follow the motion, twisting and bending at the wrist. Maintain a continuous motion by bringing your hands toward your chest while bending outward at the elbows.

2. **Hands pass under armpits:** As the hands come closer to the body, keep the palms facing up and the hands pointing in toward each other. With the full extension of the elbows to the outside, the hands pass under the armpits (fig. 5.5). In this palms-up position, move the hands past the armpits as far as you can.

3. **Pinkies and wrists twist through a ninety-degree arc:** Keeping the palms facing upward, sweep the forearms back behind the body through an approximate ninety-degree arc so that the fingers point to the back (fig. 5.6). Lead the movement through the arc by exerting a torquing force back and outward with the little fingers and twisting the wrist. This accomplishes the full backward movement.

4. **Roundabout forward movement, palms outward:** From the extreme rear position, maintain a smooth, continuous motion as you sweep the arms out to the sides. Continue twisting at the wrists and leading with the little fingers so that the forearms and hands sweep in an arc out to the sides and up to about shoulder level, arriving there with the pinky fingers in the uppermost position and the palms facing outward. Due to the curving of the tendons, the extended arms should be somewhat bent at the elbows. Continue the forward-sweeping motion from the extremities at the sides by bending the hands forward at the wrists as you push outward with the palms. Start to curve your arms into a circular pattern with the forward movement.

5. **Hands full forward:** Feel the connections and stretching building through the scapulae, shoulders, elbows, wrists, and the joints of the pinky fingers as you maintain the curving of the tendons around the bones in the forward movement of the arms (fig. 5.7). When you reach the forward position you should still feel the twist in the wrists and pinky fingers. The palms should be pressed forward with the fingers of each hand separated by about six inches and each hand stretching toward the other. Then, in one last torquing motion, twist the wrists so that the fingers and hands

Fig. 5.4 Spiral the fingers inward and move toward the armpits.

Fig. 5.5 Move the hands under the armpits and extend back.

Fig. 5.6 Sweep the forearms back.

Fig. 5.7 Sweep the forearms to the side and forward.

rotate downward and twist the thumbs forward. Feel all the finger joints and all the fingertips stretched and energized.

6. **Grand finale—find the straight vector in the curve:** Within the curvature of the stretched tendons in the bent arms, push your arms straight forward in front of you. Stretch your hands forward, torquing the hands down and twisting the thumbs forward (fig. 5.8). Simultaneously press the chin back, sink the chest inward, round the scapulae, press the lumbars out to straighten the lower back, and lightly tilt the sacrum forward. Feel the stretch and energized connections from the fingertips through the arms, the neck, and down the spine to the sacrum. The more you try to straighten the arms, the more you will feel the pull on the lower back.

   In the final crescendo of this stretch—going for the straight vector in the curve—all the elements should be performed in synchronized harmony. The whole movement—from the first spiraling of the fingers to this last stretch—should be smooth and continuous.

7. **Return the hands to the beginning position and rest:** Return your hands to the starting position, extended in front of your chest, palms facing one another. Rest briefly, smile to the tendons, and feel chi and blood flow to them. Feel the tendons growing and becoming stronger.

8. **Repeat:** Repeat this exercise three, six, or nine times.

   Comment: By practicing the exercises up to this point in this chapter, you should be developing a sense of how to experience stretching the tendons in the movements. I have therefore streamlined the following instructions, with the understanding that the reader will execute the movements in a manner that will curve and stretch the tendons. Otherwise, the movements will not be of great value.

9. **Reverse directions:** Extend the arms in front as before. Begin by starting with the palms facing outward, that is, with the backs of the hands together. Retracing your steps, move your arms to the sides and then back behind your body.

10. **Move forward under the armpits:** From the back position, move the hands forward under the armpits (fig. 5.9). Extend the arms forward from the scapulae—create an outward twist in each hand (thumbs rotate out and downward) and a counterforce in the wrists and elbows (fig. 5.10). Try to find the straight vector in the curve as you press the arms forward.

11. **End with the crescendo:** End the forward push with crescendo. Tuck the chin back, straighten the lumbars and sacrum, then push forward to find the straight vector in the curve while rotating the hands and thumbs

(fig. 5.11). Bend the palms down and give an extra push through the palms and the outstretched fingers. Feel the pull of the tendons all the way through the arms, neck, and back.

12. **Rest and repeat:** Bring the arms back to the beginning position and rest for a moment. Repeat this movement three, six, or nine times. Then rest and observe the effects.

Fig. 5.8 Palms come to front, wrists torqued down and thumbs pushed forward.

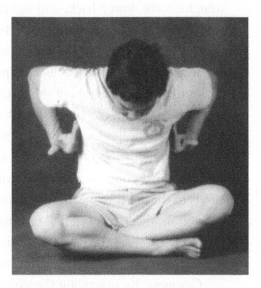

Fig. 5.9 Move the hands forward under the armpits and extend.

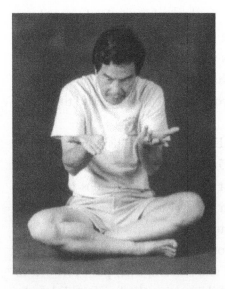

Fig. 5.10 Extend the arms forward from the scapulae.

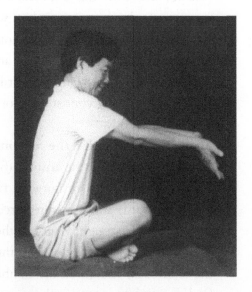

Fig. 5.11 Push the palms forward while rotating the hands and thumbs.

Short Versions of Pheasant Opens Its Wings

◎ Variation: Arms Front

The following movements are performed in front of the body and under the armpits; they don't extend back behind the body.

1. **Fingers toward chest:** Begin sitting tall, palms facing one another. Spiral the fingers in toward the chest (fig. 5.12).

2. **Fingers under armpits:** Move the upturned fingers back under the armpits (fig. 5.13).

3. **Fingers outside armpits:** This time don't extend your arms to the back. Instead, swirl the upturned fingers around to the outside under the armpits (fig. 5.14).

4. **Forearms out, palms down:** Sweep the forearms outward and turn the palms down (fig. 5.15). Finally, extend your arms straight out (in the curve), palms down.

5. **Spiral hands:** Keeping your arms extended and fingers spread, spiral your hands, bringing the pinkies up and the thumbs down (fig. 5.16).

6. **Reverse and repeat:** Now reverse directions. Starting with arms front and backs of the hands facing each other, sweep the palms out to the sides and "set the curve," except this time don't extend back past the sides of the body. Curve the wrists and hands in under the armpits and finish by extending the arms forward.

Fig. 5.12 Spiral the fingers in toward the chest.

Fig. 5.13 The fingers move back under the armpits.

Fig. 5.14 Swirl the fingers 180 degrees to the outside.

Fig. 5.15 Sweep the forearms outward and turn the palms down in order to push forward to the front again.

Fig. 5.16 The palms circle forward, wrists torqued down and thumbs forward.

❂ *Variation: Arms to the Sides and Down*

This variation begins with the hands and arms out to the sides of the body, hands close to the mat. The palms face front, thumbs pointing up.

1. **Stretch arms, turn thumbs:** Stretch the arms down toward the floor, turning the thumbs to point behind the body. Feel tension in your thumbs and up the inside of your arms. Repeat the same movement for three, six, or nine times.

2. **Spiral fingers under arms:** Now do the short version described above, starting with the backs of the hands facing ahead, thumbs pointing down. Spiral the fingers under the arms and stretch the arms downward, palms facing forward.

3. **Palms down, fingers behind:** In the final downward push, twist, and flex of the hand, feel the stretch from the heel of the palm to the fingertips. The palms face down and the fingers point behind you. Feel tension in your little finger and up the outside of your arms. Repeat three, six, or nine times.

   Comment: There is no way to really get the arms completely straight when doing this exercise. If your arms and wrists are straight you have not rotated the tendons properly. When practiced correctly there is a stretch at the shoulder, elbow, and wrist. You may be able to feel the stretch of the tendons all the way from your lower back to your fingertips. These exercises are great for enlivening the tendons.

Dragon Stretches Tail and Claws to Side
Meridians activated: Meridians of the arm—Lung, Pericardium, Heart (all yin)

This dragon is a proud creature resting on a mountainside admiring its claws. Its movements are fluid and deliberate. The dragon revels in the form and grace of movement in the twisting of its claws, as well as in the strengthening effects of the stretch produced by the twisting. It quivers ecstatically from the claw tips all the way down its spine to the tip of its tail.

Be the smiling dragon celebrating its savage beauty and raw power.

This is the first in a series of four Dragon Stretches Tail exercises; each one is identified by the orientation of the "claws." These positions stretch different sets of tendons. As in the Pheasant series that we just learned, coordinate the breath: inhale while setting the curve and exhale while finding the straight vector in the curve.

1. **Bend the elbows and raise the hands:** Begin sitting cross-legged on the mat with a tall spine. Bend your elbows and raise your hands, palms up. Lower your gaze to look at your hands—begin the exercise as a dragon admiring its wonderful lion-like claws (fig. 5.17). Anticipate the rush of peaceful energy that will surge to their very tips when you have stretched them both to the left side of your body. Imagine the counterforces you will establish at the wrists, elbows, and shoulders. Visualize the connection to the wings on your back when you have stretched your neck to the opposite side and have found the straight vector in the curve. Get ready for the final crescendo of symphonic harmony you will feel in your stretch when you connect the stretch from the tips of the claws through "the straight" to the very tip of your serpentine tail.

2. **Swing the forearms to the left:** Keeping arms and hands raised, swing the forearms to the left. Without moving your head, follow the hands with the eyes (fig. 5.18).

3. **Turn both palms to face left:** Continuing to move the hands and arms to the left, rotate the palms to face left. Begin to turn the head in the opposite direction, to the right (fig. 5.19).

4. **Turn your head to the right:** Turn your head to the right so that it completes the full twist to the right at the same time that the arms and hands complete the arc of their sweep to the left side (fig. 5.20). Make this a smooth, continuous movement as you simultaneously exhale and find the straight vector within the curve:

    1. Lightly tuck the chin, sink the chest, and round the scapulae.
    2. Rock the pelvis forward (tilt the hip bones back) and flex the lumbar vertebrae to stretch the lower back.
    3. Draw your elbows in toward each other, keeping your right elbow close to your body. Push your palms out to the left and flex your fingers back toward you. Twist the hands at the wrists so they rotate in toward each other (the left hand twists counterclockwise and right hand twists clockwise). As you twist the hands, establish the counterforces in the wrists, elbows, and shoulders to prevent the elbows from flaring out and up. Feel the tendons stretch from your fingertips to your lower back.

5. **Return to center:** Inhale as you bring your arms, hands, and head back to the center starting position. Rest briefly.

6. **Repeat on the right side:** Change directions and extend your arms to the right, turning the head from the center to the left. As you turn your head, twist your arms and push your palms (fig. 5.21). Remember to keep the

elbows in and the lumbar region moving with your pelvis. Exhale as you extend and "find the straight"; inhale as you return to center. Do three, six, or nine full rounds.

Fig. 5.17 Begin the exercise admiring your "claws."

Fig. 5.18 The arms swing left, eyes follow hands.

Fig. 5.19 Rotate palms to face left, begin to rotate head to right.

Fig. 5.20 Arms full left, head full right—find the straight vector in the curve.

Fig. 5.21 Repeat on the other side.

 Dragon Stretches Tail and Claws Up

Meridians activated: Heart, Heart Constrictor (both yin)

This exercise employs a similar pattern of movement as in Dragon Stretches Tail and Claws to Side except now you raise the arms above the head.

1. **Bend the elbows and raise the hands:** Begin sitting cross-legged on the mat with a tall spine. Bend your elbows and raise your hands, palms up. Admire your wonderful claws. Now raise the arms above the head and turn the palms up, fingers pointing toward each other (fig. 5.22). Bend the elbows out to the sides so that the backs of the hands are about six inches above the head and the fingers are separated by about six inches.

2. **Find the straight vector in the curve:**
   1. Lower your head to center and lightly tuck your chin. Roll the eyes up so that the inner gaze is directed up through the crown.
   2. Rock the pelvis forward (tilt the hip bones back) and flex the lumbar vertebrae to stretch the lower back.
   3. Pull your elbows back and twist the thumbs up and the little fingers down, creating tension as you push your palms upward. As you twist the hands, establish the counterforces in the wrists, elbows, and shoulders. Feel the tendons stretch from your fingertips to your lower back.

3. **Twist the arms and press up:** Stretch your neck, lumbar, and thoracic muscles, causing a slight rocking motion in the pelvis. Since the tendons

Tao Yin Exercises

164

Fig. 5.22 Raise arms and hands overhead, palms up.

are interconnected, you can pull your back up by pushing your palms toward the ceiling, as long as you keep your elbows back.

4. **Repeat:** Repeat this sequence three, six, or nine times. Rest and appreciate the peaceful energy surges in your body.

Comment: In this movement you want to try to straighten the arms, but the wrist twist and the elbow position will not allow the arms to straighten. The tendon stretch should run up the inside of your arms into your shoulders and all the way down your back. Exhale as you push up and inhale as you bend your arms and release the stretch. Always keep your palms facing the ceiling and your pinky fingers pointing to each other, wrists flexed and stretching.

 Dragon Stretches Tail and Claws to Both Sides
Meridians activated: Meridians of the arm—Lung, Pericardium, Heart (all yin)

1. **Bend the elbows and raise the hands:** Begin sitting cross-legged on the mat with a tall spine. Bend your elbows and raise your hands, palms up. Admire your wonderful claws. Now move your arms out to the sides like wings, palms up and elbows slightly bent. Pull your arms back slightly, opening your rib cage.

Set 5: Growing the Tendons

2. **Twist thumbs up and away:** Set up the curve by twisting the thumbs up and away from the body, with the fingers and palms following (fig. 5.23). The extended palms face out to the sides in a vertical position, the fingers pointing up. Feel the twist from the hands to the wrists, the elbows, and up to the shoulders.

3. **Find the straight vector in the curve:**
   1. Lightly tuck the chin.
   2. Rock the pelvis forward (tilt the hip bones back) and flex the lumbar vertebrae to stretch the lower back.
   3. Slowly stretch your arms away from the body, leading with the heels of the palms with the fingers flexed back. Exhale as you push and continue to rotate the palms; twist the thumbs downward and to the back so that the fingers finally point down (the left hand twists counterclockwise and right hand twists clockwise) (fig. 5.24). Feel your chest stretch and open more. Maintain the counterforces at the joints to keep them open. Feel the tendons stretch from your fingertips to your lower back.

4. **Release all tension:** Inhale golden, energizing light into the joints, tendons, and muscles as you return your arms back to the beginning position, palms up. Pause and relax.

5. **Repeat:** Do this sequence three, six, or nine rounds.

Fig. 5.23 Set up the curve: rotate the palms up and out.

Fig. 5.24 Find the straight vector in the curve.

 ## Dragon Stretches Tail and Claws to Front
Meridians activated: Meridians of arm—Lung, Pericardium, Heart (all yin)

1. **Bend the elbows and raise the hands:** Begin sitting cross-legged on the mat with a tall spine. Bend your elbows and raise your hands, palms up. Admire your wonderful claws. Now move your arms out in front of you at shoulder level, palms in. Circle your arms as if you were holding a big beach ball, but the ball is too big to reach all the way around—the fingers are separated by about six inches. Your palms should be almost facing your chest but slightly out. Your fingertips point at each other.

2. **Twist thumbs in and down:** Set up the curve in the tendons by twisting the thumbs in and down until your palms face forward (fig. 5.25).

3. **Find the straight vector in the curve:**

   1. Lightly tuck the chin to straighten the back of the neck, sink the chest, and round the scapulae.

   2. Rock the pelvis forward (tilt the hip bones back) and flex the lumbar vertebrae to stretch the lower back.

   3. Exhale and extend your arms out. Gently push your palms forward, stretching open your fingers. Simultaneously twist the thumbs downward and your little fingers upward with the counterforces at the wrists and elbows. Push all the way from the scapulae. At the same time, press the thumbs forward a little more. As you twist the hands, establish the counterforces in the wrists, elbows, and shoulders. Feel the tendons stretch from your fingertips to your lower back.

Fig. 5.25 Circle the arms front and rotate palms out to set up the curve.

4. **Release all tension:** Relax, turn your palms back in toward you, head rocking slightly back, and return to the ball-holding position. Observe the sensations in your body.

5. **Repeat:** Do this sequence three, six, or nine times.

Comment: This subtle movement is an easy one that you can do every day to stretch and grow the tendons. Just exhale and push out, inhale and relax back in with a slight rocking motion.

 ## Pull Bow and Shoot the Arrow

Practice Pull Bow and Shoot the Arrow as if you were a stealthy hunter—with all your senses at maximum awareness. Your careful movements serve to bring you closer to success. You are poised with the bow and arrow in your hands. Out of the corner of your eye you catch a blur of motion; there's a flutter of sound. If you move your head first, you lose the opportunity to shoot the arrow. With disciplined restraint, you begin the slow, stealthy sweeping movement you've rehearsed in the Dragon Stretches Tails and Claws movement. Your ingrained archer's sense is aimed at the target. Every tendon is tensed just so. At just the right moment you let the arrow fly. Your body and breath release the tension. The hunt is over.

This exercise will help open the chest, shoulders, and scapulae, and will help develop their tendons.

1. **Begin with the Dragon Stretches Tail and Claws Up:** Begin this exercise with a few rounds of Dragon Stretches Tail and Claws Up. Feel the stretch and the counterforces. Feel the connection from the fingers to the scapulae, slowly turning the palms inward as you lower the arms to the beginning Dragon position. Keep the curve in the tendons by holding the counterforces.

2. **Prepare the bow to shoot left:** Fold the pinky, ring, and middle fingers of both hands in from the second knuckle. Place your right hand a few inches away from your chest in front of your sternum. Slightly round your shoulders and rotate the right hand so that the thumb turns outward and the index finger points to the left (fig. 5.26).

3. **Extend left arm:** Point your left index finger up and extend the thumb back, palm facing outward to the left (fig. 5.27).

4. **Bend forward and rotate left:** Initiating the movement from the lower lumbars, bend forward. Then slowly begin to turn from the lower lumbar to the left, vertebra by vertebra (fig. 5.28).

5. **Twist through the upper thoracics:** Continue the spinal rotation through the upper thoracics (fig. 5.29).

6. **Rotate neck and head, pull the bowstring:** Continue the spinal rotation through the cervical spine and finally turn the head. Look up to see behind you out of the corner of your eye. Push your right shoulder slightly forward and pull your left shoulder slightly back. Inhale as you pull your left arm back and push your palm out slightly so that you feel the twist of your arm. Simultaneously pull your right arm back, as if you were pulling a bowstring (fig. 5.30).

7. **Open the chest:** Next, stretch open the shoulders to further pull the bow (fig. 5.31). The final pulling force comes from the scapulae; open the scapulae by pulling them back and closer together on each side of the spine while keeping the arms still and tensed. It is primarily your chest, shoulders, and scapulae that move; the arm movement is slight. However, your elbows should be pulled back past your armpits in the final position.

8. **Release the arrow and exhale:** Release the pull and all the tension in the scapulae. Relax and return to the center resting position.

9. **Change sides:** Repeat the exercise on the right side (fig. 5.32). Do three, six, or nine rounds.

10. **Rest:** Now rest, observing the chi flowing to the tendons.

Fig. 5.26 Prepare the bow to shoot left.

Fig. 5.27 Move your left arm to the left, rotate palm to the left.

Fig. 5.28 Bend forward from the lower lumbars and rotate left.

Fig. 5.29 Continue the rotation through the upper thoracics.

Fig. 5.30 Turn the neck and head last; begin to pull the bow.

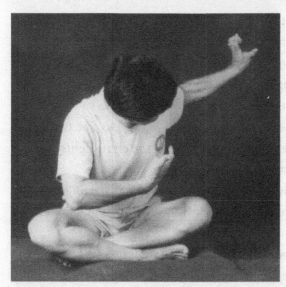

Fig. 5.31 Final upward spinal twist position—make the final pull of the bow from the scapulae.

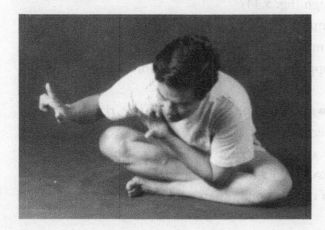

Fig. 5.32 Pull Bow and Shoot the Arrow on the right side

Bamboo Swinging in the Wind
Meridian activated: Gall Bladder (yang)

Bamboo Swinging in the Wind is yet another fine example of how an observation from nature can be transposed into a human activity in support of self-healing. In this exercise your upper body becomes the bamboo stalk/trunk and your breath becomes the wind. The upper body descends with the exhaling wind down to one side and sweeps to the other side with the blowing wind in a nearly horizontal plane. Then, as in an updraft, the inhaling wind lifts the strong, supple bamboo upright. There is a brief pause before the bamboo and wind continue their dance.

Discover the grace of moving wood and wind, body movement and breath united.

1. **Bend the left leg in front:** Sitting tall on the mat, bend the left leg so that the sole of your left foot rests against your right thigh; bend the right leg out to the side and behind you so that your right heel comes close to your buttocks. Hold your right ankle with your right hand and your left ankle with your left hand. Rotate through the lumbar spine so your entire upper body is facing out over your left leg (fig. 5.33). Do not twist your upper back at all—just rotate at the lumbars. Tuck the chin slightly so that the head cannot lead the motion.

   Comment: Figures 5.34 and 5.35 show the movement starting with the right leg to the front. The relative body position is the same with left leg in front.

2. **Lower the upper body over the front leg:** Exhaling and keeping the spine straight, lower your upper body over your left leg until your belly nearly touches your thigh (fig. 5.34).

3. **Swing outside:** Continuing the exhale, move your torso as far left as possible, letting the movement come from the lumbar spine (fig. 5.35). The hands on the ankles support the movement with coordinated pulling and pushing.

4. **Rotate right and upward:** Now begin rotating to the right, breathing normally. The movement begins in the lumbars and moves progressively through the thoracics and the cervical vertebrae; the head moves last. Again, use the hands to support the movement. At the maximum twist, hold the position for a moment and observe the spinal twist from inside (fig. 5.36).

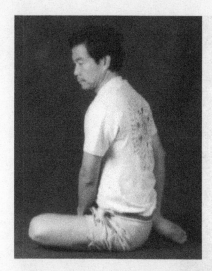

Fig. 5.33 Bend left leg in front, right leg to right side. Hold ankles and twist lower lumbars to face out over the left thigh.

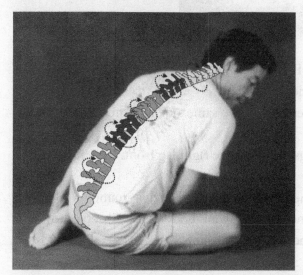

Fig. 5.34 Bend forward over the front leg, keeping the spine nearly straight.

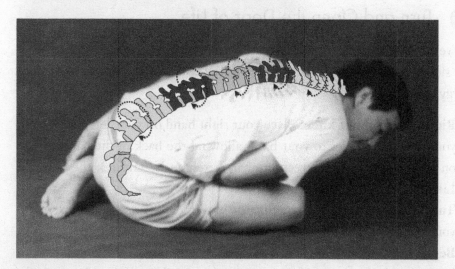

Fig. 5.35 Move horizontally toward the front leg.

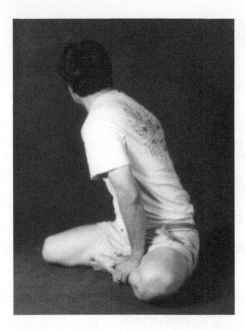

Fig. 5.36 Rotate from the lumbars upward to the right.

5. **Return back to center:** Return to center by moving from the lower tan tien, as in the Peacock series.

6. **Repeat:** Repeat the movement on the same side and then rest. Smile to the lumbars.

7. **Change legs:** Change legs, bringing the right leg front. Repeat two times on this side, then rest.

8. **Shake your spine:** When you have completed a round of Bamboo Swinging in the Wind, notice how your body feels. Observe how this movement has created openness in the spine.

⟳ Turn and Open the Door of Life

As I've noted before, the Door of Life is the lumbar area, Open the Door of Life slowly and firmly, with a smiling awareness. This exercise activates the energy of the kidneys.

1. **Right hand on left knee:** Place your right hand on your left knee. Wrap your left arm around to your back, allowing the back of the hand to rest on your lower spine between lumbar vertebrae L2 and L3, the Door of Life.

2. **Turn upper body right:** Initiating the movement from the lumbars, rotate your upper body to the right, then bend forward slightly (fig. 5.37).

3. **Begin rotation left:** From this position, begin a slow rotation to the left, beginning the movement from your lumbars while pulling with your right

arm to help the lower lumbars to rotate. Continue twisting to the left, letting the rotation move up your spine to your shoulders.

4. **Lift body upright:** Gradually lift your body to the upright position. Move your head last (fig. 5.38). Once your spine is fully twisted to the left and you are sitting up, relax back to a centered position. The movement should flow in smooth, circular arcs—rotating first to the right, bending down, twisting to the left, coming up, and then relaxing in the center.

5. **Change sides:** Place your left hand on your right knee and your right hand on your lumbar spine. Repeat the movement in the other direction, starting to the left and circling to the right.

Comment: Turn and Open the Door of Life can give you an accurate sense of the flexibility and strength of your lower back, the lumbar region. By placing the fingertips of the back hand in the spaces between lumbar vertebrae L1 and L2, L2 and L3, L3 and L4, and L4 and L5 as you bend and turn, you will feel these spaces opening and the vertebrae twisting.

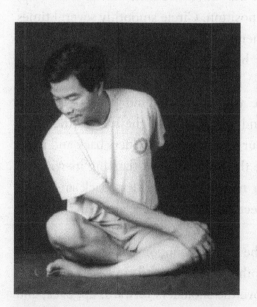

Fig. 5.37 With right hand on left knee, back of left hand on Door of Life, turn right from the lumbars and bend forward slightly.

Fig. 5.38 "Open the Door" left—rotate left from the lumbars and upward through the spine.

Hummingbird

Meridians activated: Meridians of the chest—Lung (yin) and Large Intestine (yang)

The hummingbird is so tiny and so light and its wings beat so quickly! Find the lightness in your movements. This simple movement helps release tight shoulders.

1. **Rotate shoulders one at a time:** Relax your shoulders and arms, letting your hands rest comfortably in your lap. Draw a smooth circle with your right shoulder, pushing the shoulder forward, then up, then around to the back and down. Continue around several times, concentrating on using only the one shoulder to move—try to resist any movements in your back, head, or the other shoulder. Change directions and continue for several more revolutions before switching sides. Then switch to the left shoulder.

2. **Rotate shoulders simultaneously:** After you have rotated your shoulders individually in both directions, relax and begin rotating both shoulders at once. In a smooth, circular motion, move them forward, then up, then back and down to a relaxed position. Circle smoothly several times and then switch directions. Remember that you are just moving your shoulders. Let the rest of your body be relaxed and supporting the movement.

3. **Flap wings behind back:** Place your hands behind your back, arms relaxed, palms facing out, one hand gently holding the back of the other (fig. 5.39). Rhythmically move your (now loose) shoulders back and forth (fig. 5.40). This movement is like the hummingbird flapping its wings—keep that image in mind as you move your shoulders back and forth rhythmically. Keep your spine erect and your arms relaxed, and let your chest expand and contract easily.

4. **Flap wings and rotate:** When the flapping motion has become smooth and comfortable, begin moving both shoulders in full circles as you did at the beginning of the exercise. Move the shoulders forward, up, back, and down, holding your hands behind your back, arms relaxed. Change directions after several rotations. Keep the movement loose, remembering to move from the shoulders and to let the chest respond naturally. As you move, let your pelvis rock back and forth slightly, staying loose and flexible.

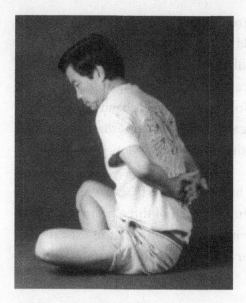

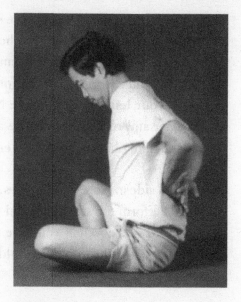

Fig. 5.39 Clasp one hand with the other behind your back.

Fig. 5.40 "Flap" your shoulders rhythmically, then move the shoulder in full circles.

 Bear Stretches Its Back

Big bear! With a mighty breath and such ponderous strength!

In this exercise, exhale slowly and powerfully like the bear. Slowly but powerfully pull the bear's shoulder back, while at the same time pulling in the opposite direction with the bear's brawny arm. Then inhale and release the counterforces. Feel the magnificent suffusion of the big bear's gentle expanding chi through the shoulder girdle and filling the crown with pleasant, soothing peace.

1. **Lean right:** Sitting cross-legged on the mat, place your right palm on the mat near your right hip. Lock your elbow and lean from the hips to give weight to the arm.
2. **Reach across chest:** With your left arm, reach across your chest, grasping your right arm at the elbow (fig. 5.41).
3. **Pull across with your left arm:** As you exhale, pull in across your body with your left arm and shoulder as you pull back with your right shoulder. These opposing forces stretch and strengthen your shoulder. Let your torso and head turn as you pull your right shoulder back; your head will naturally follow the body.

Set 5: Growing the Tendons

4. **Release and repeat:** Release the stretch and repeat several times.

5. **Move your left hand up:** Now hold your right arm just below the shoulder joint. Repeat the exercise, simultaneously pulling with left arm and shoulder and exerting a counterforce pull in the right shoulder (fig. 5.42).

6. **Move your left hand up again:** Now place your left hand on your right shoulder and repeat the exercise again. Remember to exhale as you pull your shoulder back and let your entire upper body follow your shoulder's power.

7. **Switch sides:** Now switch sides, bringing your right arm across your body. Perform the stretch several times in each of three positions.

8. **Rest and relax:** When you have completed a full round of exercises on both sides, breathe into the shoulders and observe the sensations in them.

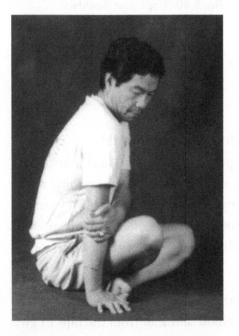

Fig. 5.41 Reach across your chest with your left arm to grasp the right arm at the elbow.

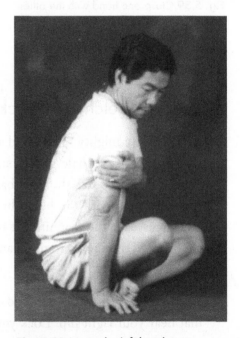

Fig. 5.42 Move the left hand up to below the shoulder. Repeat the counterforce pull.

Snake Coils around Tree
Meridian activated: Gall Bladder (yang)

On observing a snake as it coils around a tree, it is easy to see the muscles beneath its skin. The muscles are very strong but their strength is not a forced strength. In doing this exercise, sense your spine as being like a snake. As you exert the pull on the leg and begin twisting from the lumbars in the lower back, see the rippling coils of the snake from inside your spine. Just like the snake, you are naturally "coiling" without forcing the movement. Go slowly and find the snake's strength in your spinal column.

1. **Extend left leg:** Sit on the floor with your left leg extended straight in front of you. Cross your right leg over your left and place your foot on the floor just above the left knee. Wrap both hands around the bent right knee, left hand above the right. Your left hand holds the outside of the leg and the right hand holds the inside (fig. 5.43).

2. **Inhale and rotate left:** Initiating the movement from your lower lumbars, rotate to your left, successively twisting up the spine through your thoracics and into the shoulder area. Continue through the cervical vertebrae and finish by turning the head last (fig. 5.44).

3. **Rotate right:** Pull your right knee in toward your chest, then exhale as you rotate back to center and then to the right. Initiate the movement with your lower lumbar vertebra (L5) first, continuing to twist up the spine through your thoracics, your shoulders, and finally through your neck and head. Remember to keep your left leg relaxed and the foot pointing up.

4. **Return to center:** Return back to center on an inhale, before the twisting becomes uncomfortable.

5. **Repeat and reverse:** Repeat several times in this direction, then switch sides and repeat several times (fig. 5.45).

6. **Rest:** When you've completed several rounds on each side, rest and appreciate the feeling of awakened chi moving through your spine.

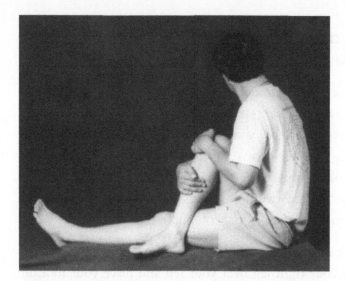

Fig. 5.43 The left leg is extended, right knee to chest.

Fig. 5.44 Do a full twist to the right.

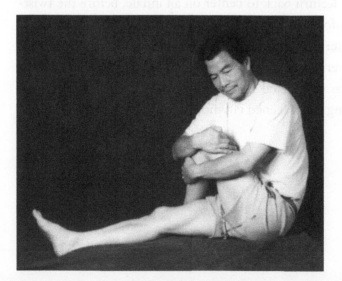

Fig. 5.45 Switch legs.

Swimming Dragon

It is rare to observe a swimming dragon. However, it is easy to imagine the powerfully flowing, flexible spine and tail propelling this mythical creature effortlessly through the water's depths. Let your spine be loose as you press your palms and flex each of the twenty-four segments of the spinal column in wavelike motions. You are the smiling swimming dragon!

1. **Place palms together, elbows out:** Sitting cross-legged on the mat, bring your palms together at heart level, elbows out to the sides (fig. 5.46). Press your palms together and feel the pressure through your hands, wrists, arms, shoulders, and scapulae all the way to the spine.
2. **Rock your spine side to side:** Gently rock your spine from side to side. Let your hands move from side to side too, hands pressing in the direction of the movement (fig. 5.47). Resist with the other hand. Initiate the movement from the Wing point.
3. **Move from heart area upward:** Using the wavelike motion, successively lift the hands higher, all the way to above the crown (fig. 5.48). Then move the hands down in the same manner, until the movement is intiated from the lower spine. Continuining with the sideways rocking motion, complete the cycle by moving the hands back up the spine to the starting position at the heart center.
4. **Circle at crown:** When your hands reach the uppermost position above your crown, you can incorporate a circling motion into the side-to-side movement, keeping the elbows wide. Move your spine in a clockwise circle and keep your hands close to the body during the movement.
5. **Hands to forehead:** Bring your hands down to forehead level (fig. 5.49). Press the palms while making another circle with your spine.
6. **Place your hands anywhere you like and make circles with your spine:** Put your hands in any position on the vertical axis, moving from your spine and pressing with your hands (figs. 5.50, 5.51, 5.52, 5.53).
7. **Repeat:** Repeat the cycle to further open and loosen the spine. Finish at the heart center (fig. 5.54).

Fig. 5.46 Press palms together at the heart.

Fig. 5.47 Rock your spine from side to side as you move your hands from side to side, letting the target segment of the spine initiate the movement.

Fig. 5.48 Move from the heart area to above the crown.

Fig. 5.49 Move hands down to forehead level.

Fig. 5.50 Bring the hands to nose level and circle at the next lower section of the cervical vertebrae.

Fig. 5.51 Continue the sideways rocking and circling through the chest area.

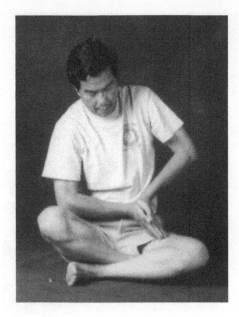

Fig. 5.52 Continue circling the spine down in the lumbar area.

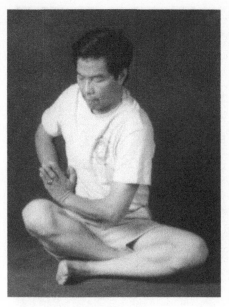

Fig. 5.53 Return the motion upward to complete the cycle.

Fig. 5.54 Finish at the heart center. Feel the spine loose, open, and relaxed.

8. **Rest:** Rest, feeling the spine loose, open, and relaxed. Enjoy the peaceful feeling in your body. Breathe in smiling golden light throughout the length of the spine.

12

Finish with Yin Meditation

A BODY FULL OF ENERGY FEELS FANTASTIC

Have fun with the Tao Yin exercises. They should feel good and create a sense of lightness in your body. Remember to practice with a smile and always keep the upper, observer mind connected to the awareness mind of the second brain in the lower tan tien. Use your Yi to move your chi.

The purpose of these exercises is to release tension and stress and to refresh and revitalize the energy of the entire being. A body full of energy feels fantastic. It is much easier to enjoy life when we feel good inside. Create a program that works for you. As in many of the Taoist practices, there are no rules, only guidelines. Use Tao Yin to support your lifestyle. Use the exercise program to create more strength, elasticity, and chi power in your body, clarity in your mind, balance in your emotions, and depth in your spirit.

Find the time and space to work on yourself. It is recommended that you do a complete Tao Yin practice, spending between half an hour to a full hour on the practice, but you must do what works for you. If that means taking five to ten minutes in the morning or before going to bed to do some simple breathing exercises, that will still be helpful. When you take time for yourself, life ceases to be a struggle. Life becomes like a river flowing down a mountain—effortless and fluid.

Keep in mind that Tao Yin is a great way to warm up the body before meditating, practicing Tai Chi Chi Kung, Simple Chi Kung, or any other form of workout you enjoy. These exercises enhance the flow of energy and enliven the body. When the body is relaxed and energized, anything you do afterward is more enjoyable.

Whether you only do a Tao Yin practice, or you do other practices beforehand or follow a Tao Yin practice with complementary practices, don't forget to finish with the yin stage of meditation. (Such other complementary practices might include the Inner Smile, Six Healing Sounds, Healing Love, Chi Nei Tsang, Microcosmic Orbit or Fusion of the Five Elements meditations, Iron Shirt Chi Kung, or Tai Chi Chi Kung.) Allow yourself some time and space for your combined efforts to culminate further, beyond the individual benefits of each part. Remember the goal of the Tao is to merge into the essential harmony of all things.

It is in the yin condition of non-doing that one is able to merge with the Wu Chi. You cannot make it happen or will it to happen. It will happen by itself when conditions are right. You must do your part to prepare the way by clearing blockages in the meridians and emotions, building strong chi in the tan tien, relaxing thoroughly, and by establishing a calm mind.

Finish your exercise session (or combined sessions) by assuming the most effective position to relax in, perhaps lying on the mat or sitting in a comfortable, supported position. During the course of your Tao Yin practice sessions, you should have had numerous "mini-yin" periods of rest between the yang, active phases of exertion. During those periods you relaxed and directed your smile and golden energizing light to the area affected by the exertion of each exercise. Accordingly, most of the meridians throughout the body have been activated with chi flow.

After a full Tao Yin session (or combined sessions), give yourself five, ten, fifteen, or more minutes, as conditions warrant, in a fully relaxed position. You have done your part by doing your practice. Now just relax. Bring all of your attention inside, letting the observer mind just observe—not react or intervene—and letting the chi flow as it will. Don't have any expectations when you begin your yin meditative session. It could be different every time. Enter it as an adventure and see what the chi brings forth.

Once you have settled yourself securely and comfortably in your relaxed position, bring a soft smile to your face. Smile to your whole body: the brain, glands, organs, spine, bones, and any area where you sense tension. Feel a fresh, soothing tingling—a healthy vibration of chi in these parts and throughout your body. Don't try to make it happen: just be aware and let it be.

Direct your attention to the lower tan tien. This area is known as the Sea of Chi, and it is the main storage area of chi in the body. Smile into the tan tien and empty your mind there. Very gently close the "lower gates" by slightly contracting the ring muscles around the sexual organs and anus; keep them closed. Stay relaxed and maintain your breath in continuous movement with a soft, slow, steady rhythm. Be aware of the rhythmic expansion and contraction of the lower abdominal area.

Sense the power of chi, perhaps like a subtle bioelectromagnetic dynamo, in the tan tien. Feel a gentle chi pressure and a slight suction in the lower abdomen. Draw the attention of your mind and eyes and other senses gently into the tan tien and keep them focused there. Feel the rhythmic ebb and flow of the subtle waves of pleasant electric chi in this Sea of Chi. Enjoy the feeling of deep inner calm and peace. That is all you have to do. Just stay alert, keep your awareness in the lower tan tien, and keep your breath moving in a soft, slow, steady rhythm for a while.

In the sense that a sea is an area of a larger ocean that extends around the world, the waves and currents in the Sea of Chi may expand and extend to other areas of the body and beyond. If you stop after a brief period, you would usually experience a pleasant quality of balanced energy permeating your body. You would feel it as a satisfying sense of peace and calm. Stay a little longer and this sensation would be of an even deeper quality. Energetically, as you maintain your breathing pattern and your relaxed focus in the tan tien, the intensity of the chi may become delightfully stronger and begin to expand.

If you decide to stop at this point, you can collect the energy in the area between the pubic bone and the rib cage. I'm deliberately using the word *collect* here: sense the area as having scattered energy that needs to first be collected into an orientation of energy that can be better managed. Do this by mentally spiraling in an outward direction around the navel in small to larger circles thirty-six times. Men begin spiraling in a clockwise direction and women begin counterclockwise.

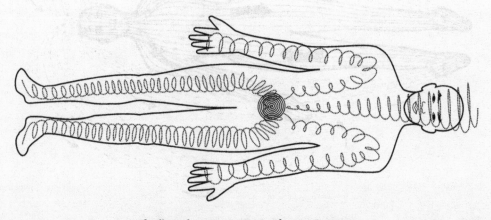

Chi flow from tan tien to the extremities

Finish with Yin
Meditation

Then reverse the direction, spiraling in the opposite direction from large to smaller circles twenty-four times to gather the chi and store it in the center of the body behind the navel. As you spiral inwardly to the navel, be aware of a funnel-shaped energy vortex with the spout entering behind the navel. You can guide the spiraling of chi energy by using your palms and eyes, or by using just the eyes. The energy gathered in this manner is condensed and stored at the energy center of the body behind the navel, about two-thirds of the distance toward the back-body wall.

As you continue in this yin meditative state there are many varieties of interesting experiences that could occur. Energetically, the electromagnetic chi dynamo in the lower tan tien may intensify the quality of chi, and the intensified chi field may expand to the middle tan tien in the chest area. As you continue the process this powerful electromagnetic chi will extend throughout the upper tan tien. The brain and the whole head will be engulfed in this dynamic field of power. It may also fill the extremities of the arms and legs with this powerful, dense quality of chi. The whole body will be imbued with this surging power. Every cell of the body will be massaged and energized with this wonderful, powerful sensation of chi movement.

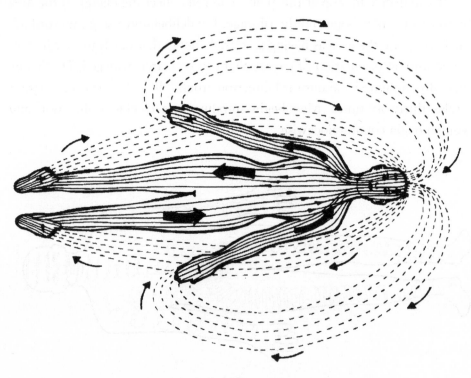

External chi-flow patterns

Then you may experience the chi flow patterns extending out around the body and reentering. These patterns may be similar to the patterns of chi flow illustrations first shown in chapter 1. This is a strong yang quality of chi experience, very pleasant and beneficial.

You might at some point experience a quite different, yin, quality of chi experience. Maintain the relaxed, soft, slow, steady breathing in the tan tien and function only as the observing witness. When conditions are right and the chi is ready, you might discover that your physical breathing has stopped for a brief period of time. This is a very quiet, subtle transition. The subtle, refined chi breathing in the tan tien connects directly with the environmental cosmic chi. The tan tien energetically functions as a chi lung. This is called inner chi breathing or embryonic breathing, Tai Hsi.

This embryonic breathing can only happen when your whole being is suffused with calm, peace, and quiet, and is at the same time full of chi. This experience may provide you with some hint of the process that enables one to merge with the Wu Chi. You cannot make this happen or will it to happen. Embryonic breathing happens by itself, when conditions are right.

Emotions are energy, too. Sometimes in this meditation, long-held emotions are released. Some emotions may have been held in subconsciously or blocked for no apparent reason. Occasionally people find themselves sobbing or laughing. If this happens to you, don't react and enter into the drama or try to figure it out. You can think about that later, if you want to. During the yin meditative state, just stay relaxed and continue to breathe in your soft, slow, steady rhythm. Only observe and maintain simple awareness.

Let the flow of energy be released without interfering; just be a relaxed witness. Whatever comes up, just let it come and go. You will be relieved and refreshed later to have the tension and subconscious anxiety removed. Interesting and pleasant things may arise as well. Likewise with any pleasant thoughts, be aware—passively enjoy, but don't react to them. Just observe.

Afterward, you may find that you have gained some valuable insights or inspiration. Sometimes you will have released incomplete or unfinished emotions that have no particular meaning or significance. You may release stagnant chi that just needs to be cleared out. Some things are processed in the Wu Chi. Afterward, it is not always necessary to understand or interpret everything you have experienced.

Usually it is best not to discuss your experience with others immediately after your yin session. It may be better for you to process your experience and keep it to yourself for awhile. Nurture the benefits within yourself before allowing yourself to be distracted by responses from others.

Finish with Yin
Meditation

Condensed Instructions for Yin Meditation

1. **Relax, attention inside, observe:** You have done your part by doing your practice. Now just relax and bring all of your attention inside, letting the observer mind just observe (not react or intervene) and let the chi flow as it will. Don't have any expectations when you begin your yin meditation session. It could be different every time. Enter it as an adventure and see what the chi brings forth.

2. **Smile to your whole body:** Smile to your brain, your glands, your organs, your spine, your bones, and any area where you sense tension. Feel a fresh, soothing tingling—a healthy vibration of chi throughout your body. Don't try to make it happen: just be aware and let it be.

3. **Close the lower gates:** Very gently close the lower gates and keep them closed by slightly contracting the ring muscles around the sexual organs and anus. Stay relaxed and maintain your breath in continuous movement with a soft, slow, steady rhythm. Be aware of the rhythmic expansion and contraction of the lower abdominal area.

Master Mantak Chia: "Do it. You'll get it!"

4. **Sense the power of tan tien chi:** Regard the chi in the tan tien as a subtle electromagnetic dynamo. Feel a gentle chi pressure and a slight suction in the lower abdomen. Draw the mind and eyes and other senses gently into the tan tien and keep them focused there. Feel the rhythmic ebb and flow of the subtle waves of pleasant electric chi in this Sea of Chi. Enjoy the feeling of deep inner calm and peace. That is all you have to do. Just stay alert, keep your awareness in the lower tan tien, and keep your breath moving in a soft, slow, steady rhythm for awhile.

5. **Collect the energy:** Conclude the session by collecting the energy in the area between the pubic bone and the rib cage. Do this by spiraling in an outward direction thirty-six times around the navel, beginning with smaller circles and drawing them increasingly larger. Then reverse the spiraling in the opposite direction, circling in large to small circles twenty-four times.

Bon voyage! Tao Yin can be used as a foundation to enter into daily life with strength and gentle power. And it can be used as a preparation for entering the Wu Chi. Yang needs yin and yin needs yang. Make it fun and enjoyable.

Finish with Yin Meditation

Appendix
The Twelve Meridians

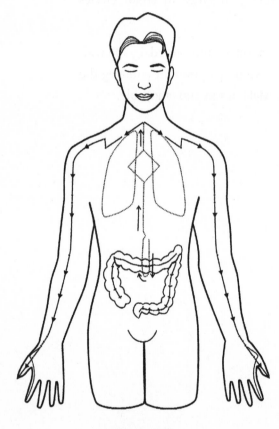

Lung meridian

Lungs

The Lung channel originates at the middle of the abdomen and travels through the arms to connect with the Large Intestine channel. From near the cauldron, it runs along the upper orifice of the stomach, passes through the diaphragm, and enters the lungs. At the portion of the lungs nearest the throat, it separates and descends along the inner aspects of the upper arms and through the forearms, ending at the inside edges of the thumbs. A branch runs directly to the inside tip of each index finger, where it links with the Large Intestine channel.

Large Intestine

The Large Intestine channel starts at the inside tips of the index fingers and runs up between the first and second metacarpal bones of each hand. Following the outer length of the forearms, it reaches the outside of the elbows, ascending along the upper arms to the highest point of the shoulders. It travels along the outer border of the acromion and culminates briefly at the C7 point. From there it descends over the shoulders, where the channel separates once again. Each half splits: one part of each route descends to connect with the lungs and diaphragm, entering the large intestine; the other part branches upward through the neck and cheek. The ascending portions travel up the sides of the mouth, partially connecting at the upper lip as they extend upward through both sides of the nose to link with the Stomach channel.

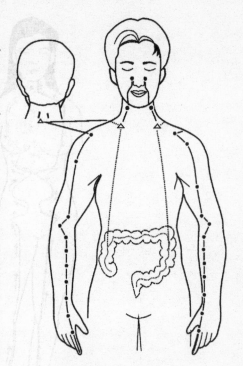

Large Intestine meridian

Stomach

The Stomach channel starts on both sides of the nose, extending almost to the inside corner of each eye. From the sides of the nose it descends over the mouth, connecting at the chin. It again separates as two branches run across the lower portion of the jaw on both sides of the head, ascending by the front of each ear along the hairline to the forehead.

Parts of these branches descend along the sides of the throat and split again near the collar bone. Two extensions pass through the diaphragm and the stomach as they travel to the groin. (The left side connects with the spleen.) The other extensions run outside, descending through the nipples and near the umbilicus on the inner sides of the lower abdomen. Four branches connect at the middle of the groin and then divide into two branches that travel down the front of the legs to the dorsal areas of the feet. These branches again split within each foot. One part extends to the outer tip of the second toe (the holding point), and the other to the inside edge of the big toe as it connects with the Spleen channel.

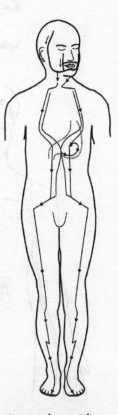

The Twelve Meridians

Stomach meridian

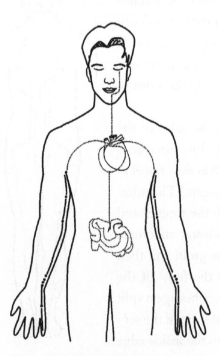

Spleen

The Spleen channel starts at the tips of the big toes, running along the insides of the feet and ascending up the legs through the inner knees and thighs. The two branches curve around the lower abdomen, combining at the navel before they split into four. One extension connects with the spleen; another flows through the stomach and into the heart to link with the Heart channel. Two remaining branches ascend through the diaphragm and along the sides of the esophagus until they reach the root of the tongue, where they culminate.

Spleen meridian

Heart

The Heart channel originates at the heart and spreads over the surrounding area, flowing down through the diaphragm to connect with the small intestine. One ascending portion of the channel runs along the center of the esophagus to connect with the eye system. Another two branches flow upward to the lungs, curving around to the insides of the forearms and flowing down through the inside edges of the pinky fingers. Here the branches link with the Small Intestine channel.

Heart meridian

Small Intestine

The Small Intestine channel starts at the outer side of the tips of the pinky fingers. Following the edges of the hands, its branches ascend up the outer sides of arms to the shoulder joints. Then they curve through the scapulae and traverse the sides of the lower neck to the front of the body, where the two branches split. Their lower extensions connect at the heart and descend as one channel, passing through the diaphragm, the stomach, and finally the small intestines. The ascending branches extend from the collar bone up the sides of the neck to the cheeks where they also split. Two extensions end at the sides of the nose near the inside corners of the eyes, where they connect with the Urinary Bladder channel. The other two extensions split further at the outside corners of the eyes and cross the cheeks to end at the ears.

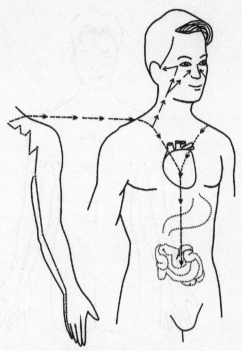

Small Intestine meridian

Urinary Bladder

The Urinary Bladder channel starts at the nose near the inside corners of the eyes. The two branches ascend to the forehead, joining at its apex, then split and run across the top of the cranium. On the back of the head the branches split again: routes descend behind the ears and converge at the back of the skull, enter the brain, reemerge, and bifurcate into two extensions of each branch. Near the base of the skull, the channel appears as four separate lines. Two of these run vertically down the insides of the scapulae, descending into the lumbar region as they enter the body cavity and connect with the kidneys and the urinary bladder. They swing back to the sacrum and descend down the inner thighs to join two other branches of the Urinary Bladder channel at the knees.

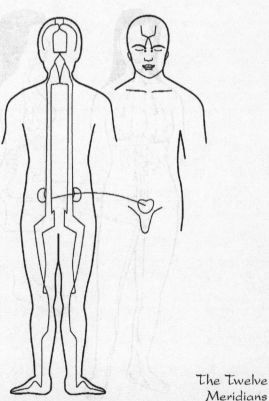

Urinary Bladder meridian

The Twelve Meridians

195

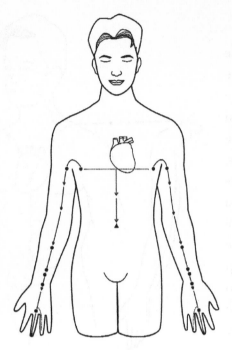

Pericardium meridian

The other two branches descend vertically from the back of the neck along the edges of the scapulae parallel to the inside channels. Passing downward through the buttocks, they cut outward and descend along the backs of the legs. From where these meet with the inside branches at the knees, the recombined lines descend along the lower legs to the outer edges of the feet, ending at the outside edges of the pinky toes. Here the branches link with the Kidney channel.

Pericardium

The Pericardium channel originates in the chest around the heart. It enters the pericardium, then it descends through the diaphragm to the abdomen. Other branches run inside the chest toward the nipples, curving up and then running down the insides of the arms to the palms. The channel ends at the tips of the middle fingers. Branches arise from the palms to connect with the Triple Warmer channel, which begins at the fourth fingers.

Kidneys

The Kidney channel starts at the underside of the little toes and runs across the soles of the feet. From the soles, the branches emerge and circulate around the protruding inner ankle bones and ascend along the inner legs and thighs toward the coccyx. From the coccyx, the channel follows the spine up to enter the kidneys. From the kidneys, two branches run down to the bladder and up through the liver and diaphragm to enter the lungs. The branches terminate at the root of the tongue. A small branch also joins the heart and links with the Pericardium channel.

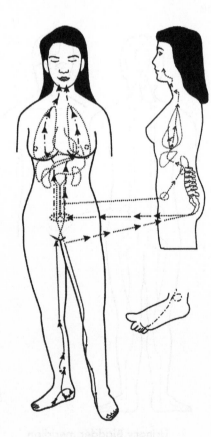

Kidney meridian

Triple Warmer

The Triple Warmer channel originates at the tip of the ring fingers, flowing across the back of each hand and ascending up the outer sides of the arms to the backs of the shoulders. Its branches wind over the shoulders to the supraclavicular fossa where they recombine and split again, spreading in the chest to connect with the pericardium before they descend through the diaphragm to the upper, middle, and lower abdomen.

A branch ascends to the supraclavicular fossa from the chest and continues over the shoulders and up the sides of the neck toward the ears. This channel splits on both sides of the neck. One branch extends around the back of the ear, up to the temple, and down to the cheek, ending at the inside corner of the eye. The other enters the ear, emerges in front of the ear, and crosses to the outer edge of the eyebrow to link with the Gall Bladder channel.

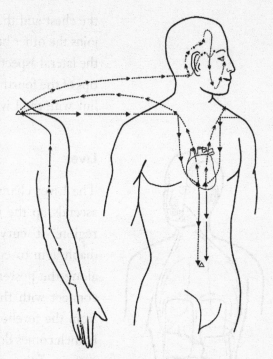

Triple Warmer meridian

Gall Bladder

The Gall Bladder channel originates in the outer canthus, flowing toward the ears, up to the corners of the forehead, and back down to the tips of the ears. Then its branches curve back around the ears, up over the cranium to the forehead, and back down the neck. They traverse the shoulders and join the other branches descending from the infraorbital regions and the cheeks at the supraclavicular fossa region.

From the supraclavicular fossa region, one branch descends into the chest and passes through the diaphragm to connect with the liver and the gall bladder. From there it runs down the abdomen, superficially along the margin of the pubic hair, and then into the hip region. The other branch runs downward along the lateral aspect of

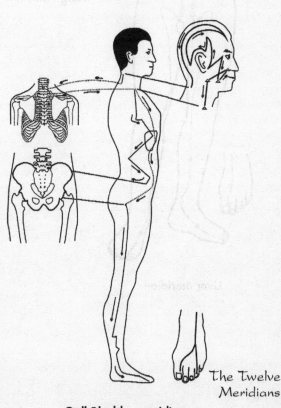

The Twelve
Meridians

Gall Bladder meridian

the chest and the free ends of the floating ribs to the hip, where it joins the other branch. The channel splits again and descends along the lateral aspects of the thighs, knees, and lower legs to the outside tips of the fourth toes. Branches also run to the big toes, where they link with the Liver channel.

Liver

The Liver channel starts at the dorsal region of the big toes and ascends up the inner sides of the knees and thighs to the pubic region. It curves around the genitalia and up through the diaphragm to curve around the chest. Then its branches ascend along the posterior aspects of the throat, crossing the cheeks to connect with the eye system. They continue upward, emerging from the forehead above the eyebrow, and pass over the head. A branch comes down from the eye system to curve around the inner surface of the upper and lower lips. Another branch arising from the liver passes through the diaphragm and lungs to link with the Lung channel.

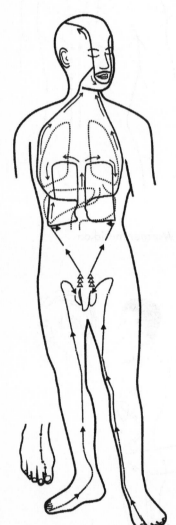

Liver meridian

About the Author

Mantak Chia has been studying the Taoist approach to life since childhood. His mastery of this ancient knowledge, enhanced by his study of other disciplines, has resulted in the development of the Universal Tao System, which is now being taught throughout the world.

Mantak Chia was born in Thailand to Chinese parents in 1944. When he was six years old, he learned from Buddhist monks how to sit and "still the mind." While in grammar school he learned traditional Thai boxing, and soon went on to acquire considerable skill in Aikido, Yoga, and Tai Chi. His studies of the Taoist way of life began in earnest when he was a student in Hong Kong, ultimately leading to his mastery of a wide variety of esoteric disciplines. To better understand the mechanisms behind healing energy, he also studied Western anatomy and medical sciences.

Master Chia has taught his system of healing and energizing practices to tens of thousands of students and trained more than two thousand instructors and practitioners throughout the world. He has established centers for Taoist study and training in many countries around the globe. In June 1990 he was honored by the International Congress of Chinese Medicine and Qi Gong (Chi Kung), which named him the Qi Gong Master of the Year.

The Universal Tao System and Training Center

THE UNIVERSAL TAO SYSTEM

The ultimate goal of Taoist practice is to transcend physical boundaries through the development of the soul and the spirit within the human. That is also the guiding principle behind the Universal Tao, a practical system of self-development that enables individuals to complete the harmonious evolution of their physical, mental, and spiritual bodies. Through a series of ancient Chinese meditative and internal energy exercises, the practitioner learns to increase physical energy, release tension, improve health, practice self-defense, and gain the ability to heal oneself and others. In the process of creating a solid foundation of health and well-being in the physical body, the practitioner also creates the basis for developing his or her spiritual potential by learning to tap into the natural energies of the sun, moon, earth, stars, and other environmental forces.

The Universal Tao practices are derived from ancient techniques rooted in the processes of nature. They have been gathered and integrated into a coherent, accessible system for well-being that works directly with the life force, or Chi, that flows through the meridian system of the body.

Master Chia has spent years developing and perfecting techniques for teaching these traditional practices to students around the world through ongoing classes, workshops, private instruction, and healing sessions, as well as books and video and audio products. Further information can be obtained at www.universal-tao.com.

THE UNIVERSAL TAO TRAINING CENTER

The Tao Garden Health Spa and Resort and Universal Tao Training Center in Chiang Mai, northern Thailand, is the home of Master Chia and serves as the worldwide headquarters for Universal Tao activities. This integrated wellness, holistic health, and training center is situated on eighty acres surrounded by the beautiful Himalayan foothills near the historic walled city of Chiang Mai. The serene setting includes flower and herb gardens ideal for meditation, open-air pavilions for practicing Chi Kung, and a health and fitness spa.

The Center offers classes year-round, as well as summer and winter retreats. It can accommodate two hundred students, and group leasing can be arranged. For more information, you may fax the Center at (66) (53) 495-852, or email universaltao@universal-tao.com.

For information worldwide on courses, books, products, and other resources, contact:

Universal Healing Tao Center
274 Moo 7, Luang Nua, Doi Saket, Chiang Mai, 50220 Thailand
Tel: (66)(53) 495-596 Fax: (66)(53) 495-852-3
Email: universaltao@universal-tao.com
Website: www.universal-tao.com

For information on retreats and Health Spa, contact:
Tao Garden Health Spa and Resort
Email: info@tao-garden.com, taogarden@hotmail.com
Website: www.tao-garden.com

Good Chi • Good Heart • Good Intention

Index